STO

7-23-73

Layman's Guide to 70 Psalms

Charles L. Taylor

Nashville   Abingdon Press   New York

LAYMAN'S GUIDE TO 70 PSALMS

Copyright © 1973 by Abingdon Press

Library of Congress Cataloging in Publication Data

Bible. O. T. Psalms. English. Taylor.
Selections. 1973. Layman's guide to 70 Psalms. 1. Bible.
O. T. Psalms—Devotional literature.
I. Taylor, Charles Lincoln, 1901-   II. Title.
BS1423.T38   223'.2   72-14228

ISBN 0-687-21221-9

MANUFACTURED BY THE PARTHENON PRESS AT
NASHVILLE, TENNESSEE, UNITED STATES OF AMERICA

Preface

Why another book about psalms of more than two thousand years ago? In sum, because they ask right questions about your life, my life, everyman's life. What is the meaning of my existence? Who am I? Whose am I? Where do I find right aims and goals? How do I live rightly with my fellow man? What do I do with suffering? How do I meet death? How can I be disinfected from self-centeredness? Whom can I trust? Where do I learn of the true God? With what language can I respond to him?

Do the Psalms give the right answers? Many of them, reflecting persecution hardly less severe than Hitler's massacre of Jews, breathe hatred of enemies and intense nationalism. No amount of pleading that we must fight the Lord's fight against sin succeeds in accommodating the hostilities of an ancient religion to Christian worship. For this reason, despite the disadvantages of selecting from any classic literature, many psalms, in whole or in part, are not presented here. Others, including some that are much cherished, have been omitted for considerations of space.

But surely we become like that to which we listen, that which we admire, that which we think about, that which we worship. Equally clear is it that the Psalms were not only the mental and spiritual food of Jesus, but have been the chief aid to Judeo-Christian devotion through the centuries. Right answers to basic questions are here if, in the midst of all the noises dinning in our ears, we can hear them.

Two specific practical concerns underlie this work. One was a desire that a particular congregation at worship should find each psalm that formed part of the service not an impediment, but an aid. A mimeographed sheet, Sunday

3

by Sunday, contained the new translation, a psalm on one side, comment and prayer on the other. The other concern was to assist the private devotion of individuals baffled as to how to use the Psalms intelligently and helpfully. They may well be read not all at once, but at the rate of one each day over a period of ten weeks.

This book is an attempt to make the Psalms' word to us more audible, then to understand it better, then to help us make the right reply. If praise and trust are marks of inner health, if all our feverish actions without love at their core are nothing worth, if God indeed is the wellspring of life worth living for both individuals and society, then the Psalms are not a relic of old times interesting only to antiquarians, but nourishment for a hungry world, and for you and me.

Key to Symbols Used

* indicates the translation omits part of the Hebrew text.
º indicates that a word or words not in Hebrew have been supplied.
G indicates that the Hebrew text reads *God.*

Phrases or lines deeply indented are likely to have been inserted into their contexts in the course of scribal copying and editing.

Contents

Psalm 1   The Two Ways

The Lord's man

1 Fortunate is the man
   who does not follow the advice of the
       wicked,
   nor stand on the street with sinners,
   nor sit in the scoffer's seat,
2 but whose delight is in the law of the Lord,
   the law which he studies day and night;
3 who is like a tree planted by the waterside
   that yields its fruit in season;
   the foliage of which does not fade;
   in whatever he does he prospers.

The wicked

4 Not so are the wicked
   who are like chaff that the wind blows
       away.

The fate of each

5 So the wicked will not endure at the judg-
       ment,
   nor sinners in the company of the just;
6 for the Lord accepts the way of the just,
   but the way of the wicked is doomed.

John Baptist said of Jesus, that he would "gather the wheat into his granary; but he will burn the chaff on a fire that can never go out" (Luke 3:17 NEB). Jesus himself made an equally sharp distinction: those who fail to help the needy "will go away to eternal punishment, but the righteous will enter eternal life" (Matt. 25:46 NEB). Both of these statements came from the same late Jewish background that produced this preface to the Psalter. The two ways, to life and death, are prominent not only in both

Old and New Testaments, but also in the Dead Sea Scrolls.

Three objections are made to this psalm, of which the most important is its view of rewards and punishment. The correlation between goodness and prosperity, sin and doom—the good man prospering in whatever he undertakes, the sinner blown away with the wind—is too remote from observable facts and is effectively challenged in the Old Testament itself (e.g., Pss. 49, 73). A second charge is that the good man's merit is primarily regarded in negative terms, as abstinence from evil; and a third, that his one positive virtue is study of the law. Law for many contemporary readers means a word that kills in contrast with a life-giving spirit.

Nevertheless, the choice of this piece to begin the Psalter was suitable, for all that follows depends upon the search for God not only through prophets and sages but through law. Although the psalm reaches no great height, through its prominent position it presents in a forceful way two fundamental truths: that the Lord is with the just, and that the man who diligently seeks and then follows the divine will is fortunate—not happy in any superficial sense, not merely lucky, but in that right state often described as blessed.

O God, on whose path the just find life, help us so to study your will, that having been found faithful to your guidance, we may stand firm under your judgment.

Psalm 2   The Divine Laughter

Rebellious nations

1 Why do the nations throng in an uproar and the peoples growl empty threats?

2 The kings of the earth rise in revolt*
   against the Lord and his anointed:
3 "Let us cut their bonds in pieces
   and cast off their ropes from us."

Divine control

4 He who dwells in the heavens laughs,
   the Lord makes sport of them;
5 then he threatens them in his anger
   and terrifies them in his fury:
6 "I have established my king
   on Zion my holy mountain."

Commission to the king

7 *He said to me, "You are my son,
   today I have adopted you.
8 Ask* the nations for your inheritance
   and the ends of the earth for your domain.
9 You shall crush them with an iron rod,
   smash them to bits like a piece of pottery."

Advice to the enemies

10 Now, therefore, kings, be prudent,
   take advice, you who rule on earth.
11 Serve the Lord with fear
   and with trembling¹² kiss his feet,
   lest he be angry and you perish*
   for his wrath is quickly kindled.

Fortunate are all who take
refuge in him.

The initial letters of the first ten lines of this psalm
spell "To Jannaeus and his wife"—Jannaeus the priest king
of Judea, Alexandra his wife, who were married in 103 B.C.

The importance of Psalm 2 for the Christian church has
rested upon a supposed reference to Christ in vs. 7 (also in
a mutilated text that reads literally, but incorrectly, "kiss
son," vs. 12) and the extensive use of the psalm in the New
Testament. It represents, however, one of the most national-

istic, vindictive, and militaristic of the Psalter.

Does God subject all nations to a warlike king to be smashed to bits? Is God quick or slow to anger? And what is to be made of the divine derision? Does a divine Father, like a human parent, laugh at his children, and, if so, how?

That God should be spiteful or piqued, that he should mock or jeer or hold his creatures in contempt does violence to the picture of the Gospels. But it would be a sadly diluted and weak version of the Christian faith that left out the wrath of God upon the disobedient—wrath in the almost impersonal sense in which Paul uses the term—the unswerving opposition of the whole universe and of him who made it to all forms of evil. Similarly there is a sense in which the pretensions of men to escape his rule are ridiculous in God's sight. The concept of the anointed representative of the Lord, called in verse 7 his son, moves from one pole to the other in the century between Jannaeus and Jesus, from the ruler with the iron rod to the suffering servant. But the primary truth of the psalm, that God is stronger than any nations, remains constant.

O God, who gave to your Son the nations as his inheritance and the ends of the earth as his domain, we pray in his words for your kingdom to come among us, and lest our silly rebellions be smashed like pottery, grant us to fear and serve you alone.

Psalm 4   *Sleep and Rest*

*Plea
to God*

1 When I call answer me, my God who defends my right,*
   in my trouble pity me and heed my prayer.

2 You men, how long is my glory to be disgraced,

Address to men

will you love a delusion, will you worship a fraud?

3 Know that the Lord shows me wonderful devotion;

the Lord hears me when I call to him.

4 When you shake with anger at heart, do not sin;

when you feel bitter upon your bed, keep silent.

5   Offer right sacrifices
              and trust in the Lord.

Prayer of trust

6 There are many who say, "Would that we could see some good!"

Lift up over us, O Lord, the light of your face.

7 You have put more gladness into my heart than others know when their grain and wine abound.

8 Let me lie down and sleep in peace,
for you alone, O Lord, make me live securely.

The theme of this psalm, traditionally used at the last service of the day (compline) is trust; its advice is patience, its mood joy.

The author of Ephesians 4:26 found useful the advice of verse 4; the prayers of verses 1, 6, and 8 are worthy prayers; the question to the doubters of verse 2 rightly scorns empty and false idol worship. Chiefly, however the psalm endures because of the author's experience of the goodness of the Lord. God shows him wonderful devotion, hears his prayer, grants him a joy greater than that of plentiful food and drink, and permits him to lie down to sleep in peace and security.

When we run after empty idols, Lord, and spurn your glory, when we shake with anger and cherish bitterness, when we question your power to show us any good, reveal once more your wonderful devotion, putting joy into our hearts as we sleep in peace.

Psalm 8   What Is Man?

Man under God

1 O Lord our sovereign,
    how majestic is your name throughout the earth!*

3 When I see* the works of your fingers,
    moon and stars which you have made,

4 what is man, that you remember him
    or mortal man that you notice him,

5 that you make him little less than divine,
    and crown him with glory and honor?

Man over the rest of creation

6 You give him mastery over the works of your hands,
    all things you have put under his feet,

7 sheep and oxen, all of them,
    and moreover the wild beasts,

8 birds in the air and fish in the sea
    that make their way through the waters.

9 O Lord our sovereign,
    how majestic is your name throughout the earth!

What is man? In *Lear* he is described as "false of heart, light of ear, bloody of hand; hog in sloth, fox in stealth, wolf in greediness, dog in madness, lion in prey" (act III, scene 4); in *Hamlet*, "What a piece of work is a man! How noble in reason! how infinite in faculty! in form, in moving how express and admirable! in action how like an angel! in apprehension how like a God!" (act II, scene 2). He is both animal and godlike, and any view which brutalizes him by neglecting the latter or sentimentalizes him by forgetting the former does violence to the truth. Psalm 8 is a classic expression of both his weakness and his glory. As the author stands in wonder under the night sky, he realizes his tiny, transitory creatureliness, but it is that very capacity for humility that allows him the privilege of communion with the divine majesty.

What a magnificent psalm this is! How beautiful the symmetry of the two halves, and the repetition of the first verse in the last! But in the end, the psalm lives for its witness to the truth. To Hume's question about the universe, "By what right do we take this little agitation of the brain which we call thought as the clue to all this?", the answer is that only man, capable of fellowship in mind and spirit with the Creator, aware of how small he is in the immensities of interstellar space, seems to have any idea as to its meaning.

We praise you, Lord, for revealing your handiwork in your vast universe, for remembering frail man, and for crowning him with glory through your companionship.

Psalm 11 Foundations

The sure foundation, the Lord

1 In the Lord I take refuge, why do you say,*
    "Flee like a bird to your mountain,
2 for look, the wicked are bending the bow,
    they have fitted their arrow onto the string;*

3 when the foundations are being destroyed
what can the just man do?"
4 The Lord is in his holy temple,
the Lord, whose throne is in the heavens.

His just
judgment

His eyes look °upon the world,
his gaze tests mankind.
5 The Lord takes pleasure in the just,
but the man who loves violence he hates.
6 Let him rain on the wicked coals of fire,*
a scorching wind be their cup to drink.
7 For the Lord is just, a lover of just deeds;
the upright shall behold his face.

For several reasons this is an important psalm: it deals with the age-old problem of the destruction of foundations, when life is difficult, and wrong seems to have the upper hand. What are those foundations? The author would be likely to think in concrete terms—of strongholds or temple rather than community life, or moral principles, or justice, or religion; but his temptation is universal: to flee when security is threatened. It asks the right question, What to do? and gives the right answer. The just man finds his confidence in the reliable Lord. The ground of his trust is God's character and power. Without perceptible excitement or even emotion, but with almost detached, cool, matter-of-fact statements, the psalmist rests his case on God's moral governance of the universe. Evil cannot win. As in the first verse with its emphatic "in the Lord," he makes his act of faith, so in the last he receives his reward: the pure in heart see God. Sung by Mary Queen of Scots at the scaffold, this psalm exemplifies the virtue for which the psalms stand supreme—trust.

When mortals say the cause is hopeless,
and when they bid us take to flight,

When earth's foundations all are shaking,
and hosts of wicked boast their might,
Our God the Lord is in his temple,
the judge of man's far-wandering race,
With him we need no other refuge,
the pure in heart shall see his face.

Psalm 15   Ten Commandments

The
question

1 Lord, who may be your guest in your tent?
Who may dwell on your holy mountain?

The
answer
tenfold

2 He whose life is blameless, who does what
is right
and speaks truth from his heart;
3 on whose tongue there is no malice,
who does no wrong to his friend,
and casts no slur upon his neighbor.
4 In his eyes an infidel is despised,
but he honors those who worship the
Lord.
When he swears to his hurt, he does not
change.
5 He does not loan his money at interest,
and he takes no bribe against the inno-
cent.

Reward

He who does these things will never be
shaken.

This psalm, neither a hymn of praise nor a striving for
trust in the midst of suffering, consists of moral instruction
that closely resembles Isaiah 33:14-16.

There is no great poetry here, if poetry at all. Some of the more important sins are unmentioned; the psalm is neither especially comprehensive nor profound. But it takes an important step on the road to right motive balanced by corresponding right action. In raising the question, Who belongs in God's house? the author is really asking, Who lives in God's favor? The answer is: Not everybody. God's grace is not cheap. His approval comes only to those whose religious faith leads to right relation with their fellows.

O God, ever calling us to dwell in your company, pour into our hearts such devotion to you that we heed your command to deal rightly with our neighbor, through him whose love could never be shaken, our Master and Lord.

Psalm 16   Guidance for Life

The Lord, the true good

1 Protect me, O God, for in you I take refuge,
2   I say to the Lord, "You are my good.*
5 You, Lord, are my proper share and my cup,
   you maintain my lot."
6 The lines have fallen for me in pleasant places,
   indeed I have a goodly heritage.
7 I bless the Lord who gives me counsel,
   for in the night my heart instructs me.

The true security

8 I set the Lord before me continually,
   with him at my side I shall not be shaken.
9 So my mind is glad and my heart rejoices,
   my body, also, rests secure.
10 For you do not abandon me to the grave
   nor allow your saints to see the Pit.

11 You show to me the path of life,*
  in your right hand are pleasures forever.

In this beautiful psalm of trust, not only an individual, but the nation Israel, speaks. It is Israel that has received the pleasant heritage, Palestine; Israel, whose proper share, or particular God, is the Lord under whose protection it receives its good and its destiny, or cup.

The concluding verses, used in the burial office of many churches, have generally been interpreted in the light of Acts 2:25-32 and 13:35-37, and these passages in turn in the light of Jesus' resurrection. But the meaning of the psalm is plain, that the speaker will not go to the grave (Sheol, the underworld, here called also the Pit). It does not mean that he will be raised out of it. (The Vulgate Latin translation substituted *in* for *to* after *abandon* in vs. 10.)

When this has been clearly recognized, then the psalm's importance is seen to be this: the road to belief in a further life that is worth anything leads through appreciation of God's presence and goodness now. "Presence," says Angus Dun, "means possibility of communion." We are sometimes in the same room with another person, but not really in his presence because we are not communicating. Equally, persons at a distance in miles or even in years are very near, speaking to us as we to them. God, too, walks beside us on the path of life; and although the psalm at first contained no clear hope of life after death, it can and does serve those who, rejoicing in the communion it fosters, now read it in the light of fuller faith.

We bless you Lord, our highest good, for your gifts, your guidance, and your saving health, asking only for your companionship on the hard but joyful path that leads to life.

Psalm 18   The Lord in the Storm

1   I love you, O Lord, my strength

Call to
the
Lord

2 The Lord is my crag and my fortress,*
    my God, my rock in whom I take refuge,
my shield and my helping horn,
    my high tower °who saves me from vio-
        lence.
3 I call to the Lord who is worthy to be
        praised
and I am saved from my enemies.

The
human
plight
and
divine
action

4 The deadly breakers engulfed me,
    destructive torrents overwhelmed me.
5 The ropes of the grave gripped me,
    the snares of death were set to trap me.
6 In my distress I called to the Lord
    and cried for help to my God;
from his temple he heard my voice
    and my cry came to his ears.
7 Then the earth quivered and quaked,
    the foundations of the heavens trem-
        bled;*
8 smoke rose from his nostrils
    and consuming fire poured from his
        mouth.*
9 Then he bent the heavens and came down
    with thick darkness under his feet.
10 He mounted a cherub and flew
    and swooped on the wings of the wind.
11 He made darkness his pavilion around him,
    the massing of waters into clouds in the
        skies.
12 Brightness flashed before him
    with hailstones and coals of fire.

13 Then the Lord thundered from heaven
   and the Most High uttered his voice,*
14 and he shot his arrows and scattered them,
   hurled lightning and dispersed them,
15 and the bed of the sea appeared
   and the foundations of the world were
   laid bare.*

*The
rescue*

16 He sent from on high, he took me,
   he drew me out of many waters.
17 He rescued me from my powerful enemy
   and from those stronger than I who hate
   me.
18 They beset me on my calamitous day
   but the Lord was my support,
19 and he set me free in an open place,
   he rescued me, for he cared for me.*

Notable in this psalm is the description of the Lord's appearance in verses 7-15. He rides a cherub on the wings of the wind, hurls his lightning out of the dark clouds that form his pavilion, flashes hail and fiery coals, and routs the powerful enemies of his people. Seldom is there more vivid, compressed, compelling poetry than this.

The value of this psalm for worship today may be chiefly in its contribution to freedom: the Lord of the storm is not arbitrary, but uses his power to save his people. For the rest, the psalm is loved for the pictures given in striking phrases, some of which are caught up in the accompanying prayer.

All glory to the Lord—who rides on the wings of the wind, who makes thunder and lightning his servants, who rescues us from stormy waters and sets us at liberty in a broad place; to the Lord, the lamp that lightens our darkness;

*whose care makes our little lives great—to this God, to you,
O Lord, we offer our praise.*

Psalm 19   Heavens Above,
Law Within

**The
starry
heavens
above**

1 The heavens are telling the glory of God,
    the sky proclaiming his handiwork.
2 Day to day pours forth speech
    and night to night shares knowledge.

3   Nothing is spoken nor are there words;
    their voice is not heard.

4 Their sound has gone out through all the
    earth
    and their words to the end of the world.
    In them he has pitched a tent for the sun,
5 which is like a bridegroom leaving his can-
    opy,
    rejoicing like a champion running a race.
6 Its start is from one end of the heavens,
    and its circuit to their other end,
    and there is nothing hid from its heat.

**The
moral
law
within**

7 The law of the Lord is perfect, restoring life,
    the decrees of the Lord are trustworthy,
    making wise the ignorant.
8 The precepts of the Lord are just,
    rejoicing the heart;
    the command of the Lord is clear,
    enlightening the eyes.
9 The word of the Lord is pure,
    enduring forever;

the ordinances of the Lord are true,
 altogether right,

10 more desirable than gold and much fine
 gold,
 sweeter than honey, honey from the comb.

11 Moreover by them your servant is taught,
 in heeding them there is great profit.

12 Who can understand errors?
 Acquit me of secret faults.

13 Also hold back your servant from the insolent;
 let them not dominate me.
 Then shall I be blameless and free
  from any great offence.

14 Let all that I say and think please you,
  O Lord, my rock and my rescuer.

A fragment of a psalm similar to a Babylonian hymn to the sun-god Shamash (vss. 1-6) has been supplemented by verses 7-14 in different meter, in praise of the Jewish law. This combination, echoed by Kant's "starry heavens above and the moral law within," is altogether right. The beauty of nature and the commands of the Lord belong together: as a foundation for the divine revelation in words, lies the unwritten glory of the heavens, while the revelation of God in nature is incomplete until interpreted in the light of his moral requirements upon man.

In number 465 of the *Spectator* (Aug. 23, 1712), Joseph Addison paraphrased the first part of the psalm. If the psalm had done nothing more than to inspire "The spacious firmament on high," it would take high rank. It expresses magnificently delight in God's creation, then joy for the benefits brought by the law, then the need for cleansing from secret faults and pride, finally a prayer for the Lord's approval of all that the suppliant says or thinks.

Joy in the law? The modern mood seems quite different. But Jews, and many Christians, have found in the law not a burden to be borne (as Paul did) but a source of joy. Ben Sirach (Ecclus. 6:29) spoke of its fetters as a strong defense and its collar a gorgeous robe. Between the two positions of Paul and Ben Sirach, Rabbi Zadok wisely says, "Make not the Law a crown to glory (boast) in it, nor an ox to live by it."

O God whose laws are better than fine gold, and whose promises are life and light and joy, cleanse us alike from the sins of pride and ignorance, that our words and thoughts may please you, our Rock and our Rescuer.

Psalm 22 Forsaken?

A
prayer
for
rescue

1 My God, my God, why have you deserted me,
   why so far from my cry, from my anguished groans?

2 *I call by day, but you do not answer,
   and by night, but cannot rest.

3 But you are holy,
   enthroned on the praises of Israel.

4 In you our fathers trusted,
   they trusted and you rescued them.

5 To you they cried and were delivered,
   in you they trusted and were not disgraced.*

11 Be not far from me for I am in trouble.
   be near for there is none to help.*

22 Let me tell your name to my brethren,
   let me praise you in the assembly.*

Let	27 Let all the ends of the earth remember
all	and turn to the Lord,
	and let all the families of the nations
nations	worship before him.
thank	28 For dominion belongs to the Lord,
	and he rules over the nations.
the	29 Him alone let all who dwell on earth wor-
Lord	ship,
	before him bow all that go down to the dust.*

30 Let men tell of the Lord to a coming generation,

31 and proclaim his deliverance to a people
yet unborn.*

This is the psalm, so precious to the early Christain church, which seems to describe the sufferings and events of the Cross almost as vividly as the Gospels do.

The words of verse 1, "My God, my God, why have you deserted me?" are the cry of Jesus reported in Matthew 27: 46 and Mark 15:34. John 19 draws upon Psalm 22:14-16, and Mark 15 upon vss. 7, 18, and 24, in both cases verses omitted from this translation.

It is unnecessary to believe that the psalmist saw Jesus in his mind's eye as he wrote or, on the other hand, that the correspondence is purely accidental. The first Christians, for whom the Psalms were sacred scripture, naturally found in Psalm 22 a norm for the understanding of suffering by which the experience of their Master was interpreted.

In the concluding lines, Psalm 22 strikes a welcome chord of praise for the Lord's care and his international rule. But the trust expressed in verses 1-22 is no less important. After sorrow and shame can follow strength and praise; only after the Cross, the Resurrection. The connection of suffering and blessing made here had momentous consequences for good when the psalm was linked with the New Testament story, possibly first of all in the mind of Jesus himself.

In you our fathers trusted, Lord; they cried and were delivered. Why have you deserted us? Or have we deserted you? In our present troubles save us, that all the families of the earth may turn to you, for yours is the dominion forever.

Psalm 23　Shepherd and Host

The shepherd

1 With the Lord my shepherd, I lack nothing;
2   he lets me lie down in green pastures.
  He leads me beside the restful waters;
3   he restores my life;
  He guides me along the right paths
    for his name's sake.
4 Even if I walk in the valley dark as death
  I need fear no harm,

    for you are with me.
    Your rod and your staff,
      these give me comfort.

The host

5 You set a table before me
    in the sight of my foes;
  you anoint my head with oil,
    my cup is full to the brim.
6 Only bounty and devotion will pursue me
  all the days of my life,
  and my home will be the house of the Lord
    to the end of my days.

The unsurpassed psalm of trust! Short as it is, there are two clear pictures here. God the good shepherd cares for his sheep, providing for them pasturage and water, guiding them on the right paths, and when danger threatens or the valley is dark, protecting and comforting them. God the host provides a feast which foes witness but do not share.

The shepherd analogy, although somewhat foreign to us in an industrial age, in its time was well adapted to express some of man's deepest convictions about God. David, the reputed author of the psalm, had been a shepherd of Bethlehem. The use of this figure, however, as many related passages show, seems to belong chiefly to a period at least five centuries after David's time. Moreover, the term *shepherd* contains national implications, for the Lord is Israel's shepherd-king.

The fundamental truths about God that have given this psalm such high rank in the world's literature are his providence, refreshment, guidance, protection, generosity, and devotion. Outward welfare and inward confident happiness are intertwined. In the teaching of Jesus, there is a double strain. He bids man follow him where he has no place to lay his head, but also to come to him to find rest.

When we must walk through the dark valley, Lord,
be our shepherd, provider, and guide,
that we may follow the right path to your house,
where your love will fill our cup to the brim,
both now and to eternity.

Psalm 24 Glorious King

Who may
worship
the Creator?

1 The Lord owns the earth and everything in it,
the world and its inhabitants,

2 for he founded it on the seas
and established it on the rivers.
3 Who may climb the mountain of the Lord,
or who may stand in his holy place?
4 He whose hands are clean and whose mind
is pure,
who does not worship what is false,*
5 he receives a reward from the Lord
and vindication from the God who saves
him.
6 We in our time seek the Lord,
the face of the God of Jacob.

The glorious Lord

7 O you gates, lift high your heads,
raise yourselves higher, ancient doors,
that the glorious king may enter.
8 Who is this, the glorious king?
The Lord, strong and mighty,
the Lord, mighty in battle.

9 O you gates, lift high your heads,
rise higher, ancient doors,
that the glorious king may enter.
10 Who is he, this glorious king?
He, the Lord of armies,
he is the glorious king.

Modern man is not so eager as an ancient Hebrew pilgrim to climb the Lord's mountain or to stand for any length of time in his temple. But we may think of verse 3 as asking, "Who may live in favor with God?" or even, "Who makes the best use of his God-given life?" The answer given in verse 4 is one of the Bible's classic definitions of the good man, whose integrity or purity of purpose is matched by outward right actions and worthy worship.

Verses 1-2, like 3-5, are also part of the prophetic heritage, which proclaims that to the Lord belong the earth, the inhabited part of it (the world), and all its living creatures. It was he who created it in its threefold dimensions of heavens, earth, and subterranean waters. God, not man, is ultimately in control.

Verses 7-10, on the other hand, are clearly of another kind, in different meter, and may possibly be among the oldest in the Psalter. While verses 1-5 beautifully state the sovereignty of God and his moral requirements, this second poem, for all its warlike spirit, is not to be ignored. God here is alive, active, glorious, strong, and mighty, even if his strength is defined in terms of armies (hosts). When men become bookish about God, or think of him sentimentally, or leave him out of their concerns and activities, this self-forgetful praise of the "youthful" God does more to bring them to the heart of religion—worship that begins as the child of wonder and becomes the father of praise—than many an exposition of doctrine or exhortation to be good.

Come to us, triumphant Lord, through the gates of hearts wide open, for yours is the world with everything in it, yours is the kingdom and the power and the glory.

Psalm 27   Light and Aid

Under attack

1 The Lord is my light and my aid;
  whom shall I fear?
The Lord is the stronghold of my life;
  of whom shall I be afraid?
2 When evildoers attack me
  to devour my flesh,

it is they, my foes and my enemies,
who stumble and fall.
3 Although an army encamp against me,
my heart does not fear,
although a battle line rise against me,
even then I am confident.

The
shelter
of the
temple

4 One thing I ask of the Lord,
that do I seek:*
to behold the beauty of the Lord
and to worship in his temple.
5 For he hides me in his shelter
on the day of trouble;
he conceals me under the cover of his tent,
on a rock he sets me high.
6 Now therefore my head is raised
over my enemies around me,
that I may offer in his tent
sacrifices with shout of praise.

Shout of
praise

Let me sing and play to the Lord.

Prayer
for
aid

7 Hear, O Lord, my voice when I cry,
pity me and answer me.
8 My mind has spoken for you,
"Seek my face."
Your face, Lord, do I seek,
9   do not hide it* from me.
Do not cast off your servant in anger;
you have been my helper;
do not abandon nor forsake me,
my God who comes to my aid.
10 Although my father and mother forsake me,
the Lord cares for me.
11 Teach me your way, O Lord,
and lead me on a level path
because of my lurking enemies.

12 Do not give me over, O Lord,
    to the will of my foes.
  For false witnesses have risen against me,
    snorting violence.

Renewed   13 *I believe I shall see the goodness of the
confidence   Lord
      in the land of the living.
  14 *Be strong and let your heart take courage,
    and wait for the Lord!

Widely recognized as one of the most beautiful psalms, 27 gives classic expression to man's longing for the presence of God. Notice, however, that this quest of the human spirit for worth and dignity through divine fellowship does not neglect material means for its advancement. Temple and the guidance of the law are both here, and trust, despite great adversity. Faith in the Lord's care is not forged in a vacuum.

The psalm is appropriate for the burial of the dead, for although seeing "the goodness of the Lord in the land of the living" meant for the author that he would not die, both in his day and now, in life and death, man must "wait for the Lord." The Austrian novelist, Franz Kafka, in *The Castle* says that impatience is the greatest sin. Communion with the Lord now is the pledge that God can overcome not only suffering, but the last enemy also.

O Lord, our light and our stronghold, so teach us your way and fill us with trust that in the time of prosperity we may offer you our joyful praise, and in the day of trouble when all earthly helpers fail, be strong, take courage, and wait for you.

Psalm 29   Thunder

Glory **to God** **on high**	1 Ascribe to the Lord, ascribe to the Lord 2 ascribe to the Lord worship the Lord	divine beings, glory and power, the glory due his name, in holy array.
The **thunder** **storm**	3 The voice of the Lord the Lord over 4 the voice of the Lord the voice of the Lord 5 The voice of the Lord the Lord breaks 6 He makes Lebanon and Sirion 8 The voice of the Lord the Lord whirls 9 The voice of the Lord and strips	is over the waters,* immense waters, full of power, full of majesty. breaks cedars, the cedars of Lebanon. skip like a calf like a wild ox.* makes the desert whirl, the desert of Kadesh. makes the oaks writhe the forests bare.*
Peace **among** **men**	10 The Lord sat and the Lord sits 11 May the Lord give May the Lord bless	over the flood as king forever. strength to his people! his people with peace!

Over every storm, God! Perfect in its symmetry, this "psalm of the seven thunders," in its twelve middle lines, describes the rumblings of one that begins over the Mediterranean, crosses the cedars of Lebanon and Mount Hermon, then whirls into the desert. As the first four lines summon the "gods" to praise the Lord, so the last four declare his rule of power and peace on earth.

A hymn to the thunder-god Baal in the Ras Shamra literature dating from about 1500 B.C. closely resembles this psalm:

> When Baal gives forth his holy voice, . . .
> convulses the earth, . . . the mountains quake, . . .
> cedars quiver at the touch of his right hand.

The Israelites, although relatively uninterested in nature except as natural phenomena contributed to their own history, fell heir to the mythology of the Semitic world, under the stimulus of which they produced a few poems of great distinction. One could wish that there were more psalms which described God's work in earth and sea and the bright immensities of the sky. For they link the God of creation with the Lord of history. Over the storm is his purpose. Glory to God on high (vs. 1-2) is matched by peace on earth (vs. 11).

O Lord and King, God of gods, revealing your majesty in thunder, grant that as we bend before you in the storm, so we may worship you when the tumult is stilled and you bless your servants with peace.

Psalm 30   Up from the Pit

The
former
rescue

1 I praise you, Lord, for you have lifted me up,
    and not let my enemies gloat over me.
2 O Lord my God,
    I cried to you and you healed me.
3 Lord, you brought me up from death's door,
    reviving me on the brink of the Pit.
4 Sing praises to the Lord, you his saints,
    and give thanks to his holy name!

5 Though his anger is fleeting his favor is lifelong,
in the evening tarries weeping, but by
morning joy!

False
security

6 But I said in my security,
"I shall never be shaken, O Lord,
7 by your favor you have made my mountain
stand firm."
You hid your face, I was put to confusion.

Prayer
for help

8 I kept calling to you, Lord,
and made supplication to my God:
9 "What profit in my blood if I sink to the
Pit?
Does dust give you thanks or declare your
faithfulness?
10 Hear, Lord, and take pity on me,
O Lord, be my helper."

Thanks-
giving

11 You have turned my wailing into dancing,
you have put off my sackcloth, and robed
me with gladness.
12 Let my heart sing your praise without ceas-
ing,
O Lord my God, let me thank you forever.

Highly significant insights into God's character are found
in this psalm: that his love exceeds his wrath and that his
support is withdrawn even from his own people when they
consider themselves secure. Generally reckoned among the
psalms to be used by the sick, it is also a thanksgiving for
God's answer to persistent prayer. Throughout, it shows
his concern that his people shall live. As the *saints* in
verse 4 and the temple *mountain* in verse 7 suggest, what
may at first have been an individual's experience has been
given a national interpretation.

In criticism of the psalm, it is urged that it excludes life that anyone would desire after death. The bargaining of verse 9, which says in effect that if God wishes praise he must keep his people alive, sticks in some throats. On the other hand, few psalms have such a profusion of memorable metaphors in such limited space: the well, the night of weeping that gives way to singing in the morning, the strong mountain that became vulnerable when God hid his face, the dance that followed weeping, and the clothes of celebration that replaced the sackcloth. Because of the truths about God's love and man's pride encased in these vivid pictures, the psalm continues to speak.

O God, ever rescuing us from the pits into which we fall, rebuke our proud boast in our deceitful security, that your lifelong favor may bring us through our present confusion and our night of weeping become the morn of song.

Psalm 32   Sin Acknowledged

Introduction	1	Fortunate is he whose disobedience is forgiven, whose sin is covered.
A description of illness	2	Fortunate is the man to whom the Lord does not charge iniquity.*
	3	While I kept silent, my bones rotted through my continual groaning.
	4	For day and night your hand lay heavy upon me. My sap was dried up as in a summer drought.

A *confession*	5	I acknowledged my sin to you and did not hide my guilt. I said, "I will confess to the Lord my disobedience as mine." And you on your part remitted the pun- ishment for my sin.
A *prayer* *to God*	6	For this let every godly man pray to you in time of trouble, that when the great waters overflow they will not reach him. 7 You are my hiding place, you keep me from trouble.*
Advice *to men*	8	Let me instruct you and teach you the way you should go. Let me advise you and °keep my eye upon you.
	9	Do not be like a horse or mule, without understanding, needing bridle and halter to curb him or he will not come near you.
A *concluding* *observation*	10	Many are the torments of the wicked, but devotion surrounds him who trusts in the Lord.
A *concluding* *exhortation*	11	Be glad in the Lord, and rejoice, you just men, and shout for joy, all you upright at heart.

Augustine of Hippo is said to have had this, his favorite
psalm, written on the walls of the room in which he died.
Luther gave it high rank as a "Pauline" psalm. Paul had
used its opening verses in Romans 4:7-8. In the churches it
is classed as one of seven penitentials (6, 32, 38, 51, 102,
130, 143). However, in most of these psalms, although there

are prayers for deliverance, true and deep contrition is rare; 32:5, like Psalm 51, is noteworthy for that reason.

In that verse 5 three words are used: *sin* or missing the mark, *disobedience* or transgression, and *guilt* or iniquity or the consequence of it (punishment). Nothing is said here of offense against man. As the essence of wrongdoing is alienation from God, the essence of forgiveness is the restoration of fellowship which God grants freely to the contrite who confess.

If the psalm is composite and primarily a thanksgiving for escape from death after a time of sickness, the psalmist's relief may not be primarily inward peace of conscience but outward health. But inward peace and outward health are not far apart. Three classes of people merge in this psalm into one: the fortunate are the faithful who are the forgiven.

Most merciful Father, whose great gift is forgiveness, for this we pray: a penitent heart, the relief of sin removed, your guidance even when we balk like mules, and the joy that follows acceptance of your surrounding love.

Psalm 34   Taste and See

The	1 Let me bless the Lord at all times,
Lord's	let his praise always be in my mouth.
care	2 Let me glory in the Lord,
of his	let the humble hear and be glad.
people	3 Magnify the Lord with me,
	and let us exalt his name together.
	4 I sought the Lord, and he answered me
	and rescued me from all my fears.

5 Look to him, and be radiant,
    and let not your faces be ashamed.
6 This poor man called and the Lord answered
    and saved him from all his troubles.*
8 Taste and see that the Lord is good!
    Fortunate is the man who takes refuge
    in him.*
11 Come, children, listen to me,
    let me teach you reverence for the Lord.
12 Who is the man that delights in life,
    who loves long life to enjoy prosperity?
13 Keep your tongue from evil
    and your lips from telling lies.
14 Depart from evil and do good,
    seek peace and pursue it.
15 The eyes of the Lord are toward the just
    and his ears toward their cry.*
17 When they cry, then the Lord hears
    and rescues them from all their troubles.
18 The Lord is near to the brokenhearted
    and saves those whose spirit is crushed.*

Although a logical development of thought is hardly to be expected in verses which begin with successive letters of the alphabet, the chief themes of Psalm 34 are not hard to find nor to remember. Because the Lord is on the side of right, it says, his saints have nothing to fear, while disaster, (in verses here omitted) on the other hand, will overtake the wicked. This same unrealistic view of the correspondence between virtue and reward, sin and punishment, characterizes much of the Old Testament, especially Deuteronomy and Proverbs. The didactic spirit of Proverbs is manifest also in the part of this psalm in which the teacher begs his children to heed his religious instruction. As in Proverbs, one of the chief sins here is lying and one of the principal virtues, humility, coupled with reverence for the Lord.

Some of the assertions of this psalm both Job and Jesus, in Luke 13:1-5, questioned. Its strength, however, is that the author succeeds in weaving into the alphabetic arrangement expressions that have become a precious part of the legacy of mankind.

> Let me bless the Lord at all times.
> Look to him and be radiant.
> Taste and see that the Lord is good.
> The Lord is near to the brokenhearted.

Often the humble worshiper finds help in lines like these that he fails to obtain from the great masterpieces. A ferry boat can move in waters where a clipper ship cannot.

Almighty God, whose worshipers lack nothing, grant that the contrite may look to you and be radiant, that peace makers may taste your goodness, that the fearful may take heart, the sorrowful rejoice, and the poor make many rich.

Psalm 36 *Well of Life*

The wicked

1 Transgression is pleasant in the mind of the wicked,

there is no fear of God before his eyes;

2 for he is much too deceived about himself to discover his sin, to hate it.

3 The words of his mouth are wrong and deceitful,

he has ceased to be prudent and to deal rightly.

4 He plans wrong upon his couch,

takes his stand on a road not good.*

The	5 O Lord, your devotion extends to the
devoted	heavens,
God	your faithfulness reaches the clouds.

5 O Lord, your devotion extends to the
heavens,
your faithfulness reaches the clouds.
6 Your justice is like the lofty mountains,
your right acts are a great ocean.*
7 How precious your devotion!* and mankind
takes refuge in the shadow of your wings.
8 They feast to the full on the plenty of your
house,
and you give them drink from the brook
of your delights.
9 For with you is the fountain of life,
in your light we see light.
10 Continue your devotion to those who acknowledge you,
and your saving help to the upright-
minded.*

How wonderful the delight in God expressed in verses
5-10! The line, "For with you is the fountain of life, in
your light we see light," comes close to the heart of the
psalms' devotion. Light is the sign of God's favor, life is his
most wonderful gift. Here also in verses 5 and 6 appear four
basic attributes of God: his devotion, his faithfulness, his
justice, and his right way of acting. Again here is love for
God's house, the temple, where more than physical longings
are abundantly satisfied.

The psalm is not sufficiently appreciated because many
readers fail to look beyond the first four verses. But the
method of Jesus was to accentuate the positive gifts and
opportunities of God, as for example when he echoed the
metaphors of this psalm. In Matthew 23:37 "How often
would I have gathered your children together as a hen
gathers her brood under her wings," in John 4:14 "the water
that I shall give him will become in him a spring of water

welling up to eternal life," and John 8:12 "I am the light of the world" (RSV).

Fountain of life, light of light, shine through our self-deception to cleanse us, expose us to your far-reaching justice to shame us, and fill us with your constant love to make us agents of your saving help.

Psalm 37   Wait Patiently for the Lord

Quiet con- fidence

1 Do not be vexed over the wicked
   nor envious of those who do wrong,
2 for they will quickly fade like the grass
   and wither like green herbs.
3 Trust in the Lord and do good,
   dwell in the land and enjoy security,
4 and take delight in the Lord,
   that he may give you your heart's desires.
5 Commit your way to the Lord,
   and trust in him, for he will act,
6 making your merit shine like the light,
   and your justice like the noonday.
7 Hold still for the Lord and wait patiently
      for him;
   do not be vexed at the prosperous man
   who carries out his wicked schemes
14   to bring down the poor and needy.
8 Quit anger and be done with wrath,
   do not be vexed, it leads only to harm.*
11 For the humble shall possess the land
   and enjoy abundant prosperity.*

16 Better is the little that belongs to the just
than the great wealth of the wicked.*

39 Help for the just comes from the Lord,
their refuge in time of trouble,

40 and the Lord helps and rescues them,*
saves them because they take refuge in
him.

"Blessed are the meek, for they shall inherit the earth,"
and, "All who take the sword will perish by the sword"
(Matt. 5:5; 26:52 RSV), echo verses 11 and 15 (here
omitted) of Psalm 37. Many other verses of this alphabetic,
repetitious, and hardly poetic psalm have become part of the
cherished, trustful vocabulary of Jews and Christians.

Why does God allow the wicked to thrive while the humble are suffering? Here the answer is that the good are always rewarded, the evil punished. Wait, trust, keep cool!
In a little while the Lord will act. Job and Psalms 49 and
73 represent other views on this subject.

Today the wisdom of this "wisdom" psalm does not appear to be overwise. None of Job's profundity is here; in fact,
Psalm 37 represents a position close to that of Job's friends
which that great book was written to combat. The author
seems to be singularly lacking in experience, or guilty of
wishful thinking, when he says that he has never seen a just
man deserted; and the Cross is the eternal rebuke to the
dogma that the good are always materially rewarded in this
life.

Religious language tends to present convictions in abso-
lutes. This psalm was not written for a fugitive fringe of
critical half-believers; it is for the devout. Its abiding message
is to wait patiently for the Lord, to roll care upon him, to
be calm without complaint, without heat, without despair.
As Paul so eloquently writes in II Corinthians 4:17 (NEB),
"our troubles are slight and short-lived" to be replaced by
God's glory. Replaced? Or do we see what the psalmist did

not, that the glory may come through the suffering, and that the glory is eternal? But the very fact that this author had no hope in another life throws into high relief his trust, overcoming the disappointments of experience, that God is with the man of peace.

O God, *while the ruthless who take the sword die by the sword, and the humble inherit the earth, fill us with your patience, that we may steadily walk the way you have prepared for us, uncomplaining, unenvious, and unafraid.*

Psalm 39   My Hope?

A suppressed question

1 I said, "Let me guard my ways,
    not to sin with my tongue.
  Let me put a bridle on my mouth
    while the wicked are with me."*
3 But my mind grew hot within me
    in my thought a fire was kindled:*
4 Make known to me my end, O Lord,
    and what is the length of my days.*

Is man only a passing guest?

5   Look, you have made my days as hand-
        breadths,
      and my lifetime is as nothing to you.
    Every man that stands is only a breath,
6   as a mere shadow each goes about.
    Only in vain he heaps up riches
      but does not know who will get them.

7 And now, O Lord, for what do I wait?
  My hope? it is in you.*
12 Hear my prayer, O Lord,*
  do not be silent at my tears,

> although I am your passing guest,
> a pilgrim like all my fathers.
> 13 Look away from me that I may smile
> before I go and am no more.

Underlying this psalm in its present state is a poem of extraordinary pathos. The author, in a way unusual for the psalter but characteristic of Job, reflects on the shortness and sorrow of his earthly pilgrimage. He intends not to speak openly, lest the wicked accuse him of infidelity, but privately he seeks the answer to life's riddle. He realizes how transitory his days are; he has no prospect of anything good beyond death; he is a temporary lodger upon earth who has found tears instead of happiness. What is the meaning of this life? Where can he find consolation and the assurance that it is more than ephemeral vanity?

The merit of this elegy is that its author continues to seek help from help's ultimate source. His God is at the center of his thinking, even when God is silent. His confidence matches his problem. The faith contained in the words, "O Lord, for what do I wait? My hope? It is in you," is one of the most remarkable achievements of the Old Testament. Unaided by a Christian view of life beyond the grave, faced with extinction not long to be delayed, the psalmist nevertheless recognizes where life's meaning is to be found. A world without God, as the author of Ephesians 2:12 perceived, may lose hope also.

O God, because you alone cure life's emptiness, we look to you, that amid the vanity of heaped-up riches and the shortness of our shadowy days, we may find the meaning of our pilgrimage and the dignity that belongs to your servants and your sons.

Psalm 40 I Come

Rescue

1 I waited, waited for the Lord,*
    and he paid heed to my cry,
2 and brought me out of the ruinous pit,
    out of the miry ooze,
  and set my feet upon a rock,
    making my steps secure;
3 and he put a new song into my mouth,
    praise to our God:

**The
wonder
of it**

"Let many see and stand in awe
    and put their trust in the Lord."*
5 You have done many wonderful things,
    O Lord, my God,
  and as for your purposes for us—
    none can compare with you—
  if I should declare and speak of them,
    they are too many to count.

**The true
sacrifice**

6 You have no desire for sacrifice and offer-
          ing—
    you have opened my ears—
  burnt offering and sin offering you have not
          asked;
7   then I said, "Here I come."*
8 I desire to do your will, O my God,
    and your law is within my heart.
9 *Look, I do not restrain my lips
    as you, O Lord, well know.

**The
proclama-
tion and
concluding
plea**

10 I have not hid your saving help
    within my heart,*
  I have not concealed your devotion and
        faithfulness
    from the great assembly.

> 11 You, O Lord, do not withhold
>   your acts of compassion from me.
>   Let your devotion and your faithfulness
>   constantly protect me.*

The original poem here may have had sixteen lines; very great lines they are. They pierce through the trappings of religion to the essence of God's delight and demand, which is the law of loyalty in the heart. The author of the Letter to the Hebrews could appropriately quote this psalm as he contrasted the continual offerings according to the law with the perfect sacrifice of Christ (10:5-9). As the psalmist speaks of the law and the great assembly, he is still within the temple system, but, like the authors of Psalms 50, 51, and 69:31, he joins the prophets in questioning part of that system's practice, animal sacrifice. In Psalm 40 there is a new basis for religion—the heart's obedience—which leads to a new security, a new song, and what the author of Jeremiah 31:31-34 called a new covenant.

Is the author speaking for the nation in verse 5? Probably yes, but however that may be, in his attitude of the open ear, in his recognition of what kind of sacrifice pleases God, and in his proclamation of the wonderful deeds of God whom he has found in his experience, he has touched three of the fundamental rocks of religion: receptivity to God's revelation, readiness to sacrifice self in the most secret places of one's inner being, and a gospel-sharing fellowship.

Open our ears, O God, that we may hear your word, make known your saving help within our hearts, and delight our wills with your all-loving purpose, that when we have patiently waited for you and been steadied, we may proclaim your wonders to the world.

Psalms 42-43 Where Is Your God?

Longing
for the
Lord
and his
house

1 As a deer gasps
    for flowing water,
  so do I gasp
    for you, O Lord.^G

2 I thirst for the Lord,^G
    for the God of my life;
  how long till I come to see
    the face of the Lord? ^G

3 My tears have been my food
    day and night
  while men are asking me all day long,
    "Where is your God?"

4 *Let me march in the company of the great
    to the house of the Lord,^G
  with the joyful cry of thanksgiving,
    a multitude keeping festival.

5 Why am I so downcast,
    and why do I groan within me?
  Count on the Lord,^G for I shall thank him
    still,
  my helper and my God.

Longing
for
relief
from
oppres-
sion
and
scorn

6 My heart is downcast within me,
    therefore I remember you,
  though far from the land of Jordan and
    Hermon
    and the Little Mountain.

7 Deep calls to deep
    at the roar of your cataracts,
  all your breakers and waves
    roll over me.*

45

9 Let me say to the Lord,[G] my rock,
"Why have you forgotten me,
why must I walk in gloom
while an enemy oppresses me?"
10 As with torture in my bones
my foes taunt me,
while they are asking me all day long,
"Where is your God?"
11 Why am I so downcast,
and why do I groan within me?
Count on the Lord,[G] for I shall thank him
still,
my helper and my God.

Longing 43:1 Vindicate me and plead my cause,
for   against an ungodly nation,
vindica-   from the deceitful and wicked man,
tion   O Lord,[G] you will deliver me.
and the 2 For you, O Lord,[G] are my refuge,
temple   why have you abandoned me?
Why must I wander in gloom
while an enemy oppresses me?
3 Send out your light and your faithfulness;
let these lead me,
let them bring me to your holy mountain
and to your dwelling,
4 that I may come to your altar, O Lord,[G]
to the God of my joy,
and rejoice and thank you upon the harp,
O Lord,[G] my God.
5 Why am I so downcast,
and why do I groan within me?
Count on the Lord,[G] for I shall thank him
still,
my helper and my God.

The theme of this poem, one of the most beautiful in the psalter, is the trustful longing of an absentee for the worship of the temple and, through the temple, for God himself. No psalmist hesitated to use the phrase "see the face of the Lord" for attendance at worship.

Problems of interpretation give rise to many speculations about this psalm. What, for example, is meant by deep calling to deep? Is it the waters above the earth thundering to the waters beneath in a cataract or waterspout? Or is this figurative language, as the second line of the same verse seems to be? And where is the psalmist? What is his woe? What essentially does he say?

Is it not that even in his absence, he still plans to visit the sacred place to share in its joy and thanksgiving? It is unnecessary to assume that he is ill. Most keenly he feels loneliness in an environment of infidelity. Those about him, the ungodly in contrast with the great or noble (42:4), taunt him with the ancient equivalent of "God is dead." If only he could see God's face, i.e., keep festival! Out of his gloom, out of the storms of his life that threaten to overwhelm him, he prays that God's favor and faithfulness, half-personified, will lead him again to the joyful place. God is his life, his rock above the swirling waters, his refuge or strength, his joy, and his help. Whatever deep calling to deep means literally, through this author's love for the temple and the God found in it, the deep mysteries of the universe answer the deep secrets of the human heart.

We thank you, O God, for deep calling to deep in the mystery of life, for desire and fulfillment, for the pilgrimage and your house at the end. Send out your light to lead us in the goodly fellowship to your holy mountain, where at the last we shall know you fully, our hope and joy forever.

Psalm 46   A Mighty Fortress

Security against nature's turmoil

1 The Lord ^G is our refuge and stronghold,
    a well-proven help in trouble.
2 We fear not, therefore, though the earth dissolve,
    though the mountains totter in the heart of the sea;
3 let its waters rage and foam,
    let the mountains shake at its violence.

    ºThe Lord of hosts is with us,
      the God of Jacob is our fortress.

Security in the threatened city

4 *His streams delight the sacred city,
    the Most High sanctifies his dwelling.
5 With the Lord ^G in her midst, may she not totter,
    may the Lord ^G help her when morning dawns.
6 Though nations rage, kingdoms totter,
    thunder resound, earth dissolve,

7   the Lord of hosts is with us,
      the God of Jacob is our fortress.

God over a warring world

8 Come, behold the works of the Lord,*
9   who makes wars cease to the end of the earth,
    breaking bow, shattering spear,
    burning shields in the fire.
10 Be still and acknowledge that I am God,
    high over the nations, high over the earth.

11   The Lord of hosts is with us,
      the God of Jacob is our fortress.

On this classic expression of trust in the midst of turmoil, Luther built his hymn, "A Mighty Fortress Is Our God." The worst that nature or man can do to God's people—the sea in ancient mythology representing the forces that contest God's power—need cause no fear. The city that he makes inviolable by his presence enjoys the only ultimate security.

The poem clearly is built in three parts of four lines each, with a refrain at the end of the second and third sections that is here restored after the first. The first shows nature in turmoil; the second adds to that turmoil the upheaval of man's making through the dissolution of his political order; the third declares God's supremacy even over the tumult of war.

A favorite psalm of pacifists, the psalm is precious to all who are looking for confidence in the midst of an unstable world. Men's thought about the manner of God's working has changed; his protection does not change. He is our fortress.

Quiet our minds and fortify our hearts, O Lord, our ever-present help in trouble, that though all nature rage and foam, all nations roar and totter, your peace may descend upon your world.

Psalm 47   Ascension

All
peoples,
praise

1 All you peoples, clap your hands,
   shout to the Lord ᴳ with joyful voice!
2 For the Lord, Most High, must be revered,
   great king over all the earth.
3 He subdues peoples under us
   and nations under our feet.

4 He chooses for us our inheritance,
   the pride of Jacob, whom he loved.

5   God has ascended with a shout,
         the Lord at the trumpet sound.

6   Sing praises to the Lord,G sing praises,
         sing praises to our king, sing praises.

The   7 For the Lord G is king of all the earth,
king   sing praises with a psalm.
over   8 The Lord G rules over the nations,
all   the Lord G sits on his holy throne.

9 The princes of the peoples gather
   with ᵒthe people of the God of Abraham,

10 for the shields of the earth belong to the
   Lord G;
   he is highly exalted ᵒabove all gods.

What is meant by the word *ascended* in verse 5? Did God ascend a throne? or the temple hill? or heaven after having come down to win victory in battle? Or is this word only a "phraseological relic"? As the smoke of sacrifice ascends does God rise with it?

Many are the interpretations given this psalm. An older school tried to discover in some military victory an historical background. Then this and other enthronement hymns were thought to reflect popular Near Eastern mythology: at the end of time, God will arise, slay the monsters of the abyss, and assume universal sovereignty. Then a New Year royal accession festival was assumed to have occasioned it.

What is clear is that Psalm 47, like 96–98 which it resembles, is a hymn to accompany liturgical acts in the temple worship. Sacrifice after verse 4 was likely. The psalm reflects Jewish confidence that all nations will eventually acknowledge the Lord's dominion. Its assertion that he "subdues peoples under us and nations under our feet" has not been realized, and the national pride asserted here is always dangerous, but because—in faith—the Lord rules, those who use this psalm on Ascension Day or at Rosh Hashanah find that it expresses well their joyous praise for his universal sovereignty.

O Lord, our King, ascending in majesty, ruler of rulers, governor of nations, holy and awesome God, to you alone Most High, we sing our praise.

Psalm 49 Why Fear?

Why
fear
the
rich?

*5 Why should I fear in times of trouble
    when evil persecutors surround me,
6 those who trust in their wealth
    and boast of their great riches?
7 No man can ever buy himself off
    nor pay to the Lord G his ransom,

8   the redemption of their lives is too costly

9 that he should live for ever and ever
    and never see the grave.

All
men
die

10 For anyone may see that wise men die,
    fools and dolts perish together,
    and they leave their wealth to others;
11   graves are their abode forever,
    their dwelling place for all generations,
    though lands are called by their names.
12 Man cannot abide in pomp,
    he is like the beasts that perish.*

Death
the end

16 Do not be afraid when a man grows rich,
    when the wealth of his house increases.

17 No man takes anything with him in death,
>   his wealth does not descend with him.
18 Though he counts himself fortunate while
>   he lives,
>   and men praise him in his prosperity,
19 he will join the generation of his fathers,
>   where they never see the light.
20 Man cannot abide in pomp,
>   he is like the beasts that perish.

Under the heading "Positive Meanings of Death" in his *Thoughts on Death and Life*, W. E. Hocking (New York: Harper and Brothers, 1937) asserts the necessity of death to prevent undue concentration of power, wisdom, and authority in the hands of a few, and to preserve flexibility in the life of the human race. "It is not merely that the old become static, . . . they frequently become wise and prudent." Their very wisdom prevents that adventurous spirit on which so much good for man depends. But death corrects this. "A rude mechanical justice, operating without noise, incessantly reduces to common dust all the mounting conquests of personal prowess and distributes their yield to new hands." The sanity of a race ever prone to magnify human achievement is restored.

Death the foe of human pretensions! This is the realistic, down-to-earth message of Psalm 49. As the author faces the problem of the world's injustice, why rich oppressors prosper while their victims are persecuted and afraid, he protests that the wicked, in the end, are in no better case than the good.

Man's life consists not in the abundance of things he possesses. However arrogant the rich may become, however secure, whatever applause they win from the world, whatever their glory and honor, death comes to all. God cannot be bought off. It is left for Psalms 73 and 139 to develop the positive truth that fellowship with God is life's highest good.

O God, whose Son exposed the deceitfulness of riches and declared that life is more than possessions, free us from every fear and envy, that we may prize only what is worth prizing; and when wealth allures us, deliver us from the power of hell.

Psalm 50   What God Asks

Introduc-
tion
	1 The Lord* speaks and summons the earth
	        from the rising to the setting sun.*
	4 He summons the heavens above
	        and the earth to the judging of his
	            people.*

Wrong
and
right
sacrifice
	8 Not for your sacrifices do I accuse you,
	        nor for your offerings before me
	            continually.
	9 I accept no bull from your house,
	        nor he-goats from your pens.
	10 For mine are all the beasts of the forest,
	        the cattle by thousands on the mountains.
	11 I know all the birds of the heights,
	        and the creatures that move in the field
	            are mine.
	12 If I were hungry, I should not tell you,
	        for mine is the world and everything in it.
	13 Do I eat the flesh of bulls
	        or drink the blood of goats?
	14 Make thanksgiving your sacrifice to me,
	        and perform your vows to the Most High,

15 and call upon me on the day of trouble,
    let me save you while you honor me.

Conduct 16 *What right have you to recite my statutes,
unaccept-   or take my covenant on your lips,
able 17 while you hate discipline
and   and toss my words behind you?
acceptable 18 When you see a thief, you are friendly with
with God   him,
    and with adulterers you keep company.
19 You unleash your mouth with vile talk
    and your tongue frames deceit.
20 You speak shamefully against your brother;
    you slander your own mother's son.
21 These things you have done while I kept
    silent,
    you thought that I am like yourself.*
22 Consider this, then, you who forget me,
    lest I tear you to pieces, with no one to
    save you.
23 He who makes thanksgiving his sacrifice
    honors me,
    and the upright in life I will show my
    saving help.*

Rarely do hymns challenge the value of customary religious practices. They tend to reflect, even to lag behind, popular thinking; the burden of criticism and reform is the lonely prophet's. In keeping with this general rule, only a few psalms question the adequacy of the sacrificial apparatus of Jewish religion. But Psalm 50 magnificently demands that religious piety result in right moral action.

After the introduction, the psalm falls into two parts. The first charges Israel with formalism. Not that the sacrificial system is totally abolished; verse 14 may mean: "sacrifice a thank-offering" and vows are to be paid. But the point remains: trust and gratitude, inward right attitudes, are more important in the eyes of God than any arrogant attempt of his creatures to feed him or buy his favor. The psalm has a positive as well as a negative requirement. Verse 15 has been called the key verse of the whole psalter.

The second part illustrates the connection between right religion and right morality; with man's duty towards God goes his duty towards his neighbor. The charge here is violation of the commandments that affect man's dealings with his brother man. But the person who has a right attitude toward God and is blameless towards his neighbor is promised God's saving help.

In sum, God asks man's grateful trust and acceptance of the help proffered to him, and that a man behave rightly toward those whom he has seen, if he is to be right with God whom he has not seen. In the end, says the Old Testament, the upright will see God's work; says the New, the pure in heart will see God.

God of the world and everything in it, needing no gifts but requiring more than any man, make us ill-content with the formalities of our worship and the self-seeking in our petty sacrifices, that by obedience to your commands we may honor you, and in trust and thanksgiving find your saving help.

Psalm 51   A Clean Heart

Prayer
for
forgiveness

1 Take pity on me, Lord,^G in your devotion,
     in the fulness of your mercy blot out my
          faults.
2 Wash me thoroughly from my guilt
     and cleanse me from my sin.

3 For I acknowledge my faults,
    and my sin is constantly with me.
4 Against you, you only, I have sinned,
    and done what is wrong in your sight,
  but you are just when you give sentence
    and blameless when you judge.

5 Look, in guilt I was born
    and in sin my mother conceived me,

*God's
response*

6 but you desire faithfulness in hidden places,
    and in secret you teach me wisdom.
7 You purge me with hyssop that I may be clean,
    you wash me that I may be whiter than snow.
8 You make me hear joy and gladness,
    the bones which you have crushed rejoice.

*Prayer
for
a new
spirit*

9 Hide your face from my sins,
    and blot out all my guilt.
10 Create for me a pure heart, Lord,G
    and renew a firm spirit within me.
11 Do not drive me from your presence,
    nor take your holy spirit from me.
12 Restore for me the joy of your help,
    and may a willing spirit uphold me,
13 that I may teach transgressors your ways
    and sinners may return to you.

*God's
desire*

14 Deliver me from violence,
    O Lord,G my God who saves me,
  my tongue will shout your justice*
15   and my mouth declare your praise.
16 For you do not desire sacrifice,
    if I give a burnt offering you are not pleased.
17 My sacrifice, O Lord,G is a broken spirit,
    a broken and a contrite heart.*

Psalm 51 is one of the noblest penitential hymns for at least three reasons: its teaching about inner religion, about sin, and about repentance.

"Create for me a pure heart" suggests the sixth Beatitude. Because the heart for the Hebrew is the seat of the intellect, this verse might also be translated, "Make me an unclouded mind." It also suggests integrity, which is further defined by the adjectives with the noun "spirit": firm, holy, willing, and broken, or confident, pure, voluntary, humble. Without this kind of heart, mind, and spirit, external sacrifice is nothing.

Sin, into which man is born, defiles a man, plagues him, unsettles him, grieves him, crushes him. Verse 5 does not imply any wrongdoing on the part of the mother, but only that from birth man is involved not only in wrong against his fellows, but primarily in sin against God. God is the only one who can set things right through the restoration of a broken relationship.

While God makes the new man, it is man who voluntarily permits God to set him free. When man is contrite, i.e., self-crushed, God does not have to crush him. The result is the joy of being forgiven, a sense of a new task, and a glad liberty in God's presence. Jerome's translation of verse 12, introducing into the Hebrew a thought that is not there, nevertheless expresses the prayer of Christians, "Restore for me the joy of your Jesus."

O merciful and loving God, forgiving the sins of the penitent, accepting the devotion that is offered in secret, create within us new and contrite hearts, cleanse us alike from faults seen by others and corruption known only to you, and so fill us with your spirit that through our loyalty your people may turn to your Son, Jesus Christ our Lord.

Psalm 63   Better than Life

**God
in the
sanctuary**

1 O Lord ^G my God,* I long for you,
    I am athirst for you.
  My flesh faints with desire for you,
    like parched* land without water.
2 So longing, I see you in the sanctuary,
    beholding your power and glory.

3   Because your devotion is better than life,
      my lips praise you.

4 So let me bless you as long as I live,
    while I lift up my hands in your name.

5   Because I am feasted as if with rich food,
      my mouth shouts your praise.

**God
in the
night**

6 When I remember you on my bed,
    in the night watches thinking of you,
7 because you have been my help,
    I shout for joy in the shade of your wings.
8 My whole self clings fast to you,
    your right hand supports me.*

A psalm that reaches the heights of 63 deserves to be
better known. In reading, it may be well to look first at
verses 1, 2, and 4, then 3 and 5, then 6-8, and again 3 and 5
as a refrain. In the temple the author, and many others
through the ages to the present day, have an experience of
the love, the power, and glory of God as real as the building.
In the thoughts of the night, also, man clings to God whose
devotion is better than life.

*God of power and glory, whose love has proven better
than life, in the night watches answer the thirst of our*

hearts, and in the shadow of the Cross let us find our deepest joy.

Psalm 65   A Rich Harvest

Universal praise

1 To you, O Lord,G* praise is due,
   and to you vows are paid.
2 To you, who listen to prayer,
   let all flesh come!*
5 With prosperity you answer us, God our
      savior,
      the confidence of all ends of the earth,*
7 stilling the roaring of the seas*
   and the tumult of the peoples,
8 so that distant folk revere your tokens;
   you make dawn and sunset shout for joy.

Prosperity

9 You visit the earth and water it,
   you heap riches upon it,*
10 drenching its furrows, smoothing its ridges,
   softening it with showers.*
11 You crown the year with your bounty
   while your paths overflow with plenty.
12 The pastures of the wilderness overflow
   as the hills are girded with joy.
13 The meadows are clothed with sheep,
   and the valleys are decked with grain.*

Praise and thanks belong to the Lord for the good crops with which he has brought prosperity to the earth. Moreover, because the fruits of the soil are not for any one people alone, all men are to join in thanksgiving. The word "us" in verse 5 refers to Israel, but, in the spirit of Isaiah 40–66,

Israel serves to connect all mankind with God. Its God is the confidence of those who dwell at the ends of the earth.

What a beautiful poem this is! Abundance, hope, and gratitude are its theme. The Lord makes dawn and sunset shout for joy. His tokens are in all the world. Nature joins man in his praise. Therefore let all flesh come to him and all the corners of the earth trust him.

O God of all the earth, we thank you for rain and sunshine, dawn and sunset, ripe fields and flocks and the joy of the hills at harvest. In our prosperity, when you have stilled the roaring of the sea and the tumult of the peoples, let us never forget your praise nor the prayer that to you all flesh may come.

Psalm 67   Saving Power

A harvest prayer and thanksgiving

1 The Lord G be kind to us and bless us,
  making his face to shine upon us.

3 Let the peoples thank you, Lord,G
   let the peoples, all of them, thank you,

2 that your way may be known on the earth,
  your saving power among all nations.

4 Let the nations be glad and sing for joy,
  o for you govern the world justly,
  you govern the peoples with equity
  and guide the nations on the earth.

5 Let the peoples thank you, Lord,G
   let the peoples, all of them, thank you!

6 The earth has given its increase,
  the Lord G our God blesses us.

7 May the Lord G bless us,
and all the ends of the earth revere him!

Psalm 67 is a hymn of thanksgiving for a harvest, but also a prayer that all nations may share Israel's good fortune and praise its God. God's gifts, God's rule are not confined to one people, but are universal.

There seems to have been a sacrifice or some form of ritual action between verses 5 and 6. God's favor (the shining of his face), which is sought in verses 1-5, has been granted in the next verse (the earth has given its increase), and this acknowledgment leads to a further prayer in verse 7. In this characteristic combination of gratitude and trust, the psalm articulates, in lines suitable for use on many occasions, two fundamentals of religious faith and practice.

Governor of every country upon earth, who through no merit of ours gave to our land wealth and peace, grant us grace to make known your way upon earth, your saving health among all nations, until all peoples praise you and every man is blessed, through Jesus Christ our Lord.

Psalm 71   Old Age

**The
divine
lifelong
education**

1 In you, O Lord, I take refuge,
let me never be disgraced.*
5 For you, O Lord, are my hope,
my confidence* since my youth.
6 On you I have leaned since I was born,*
and you are my constant theme of praise.
7 I have been a marvel to many,
but you are my refuge and strength.

8 My mouth is full of your praise,
 of your glory all day long.

9 Do not reject me when I am old,
 when my strength fails do not leave me.*
17 Lord,G you have taught me since my youth,
 and still I declare your wonders;
18 now also, when I am old and gray-haired,
 O Lord,G do not leave me,
 until I declare your might to a coming
 generation
19 *and your justice, Lord,G to the skies.
 You have done great deeds;
 O Lord,G who is like you?
20 You have shown me many bitter troubles
 but will revive me again,
 and from the depths of the earth
 will bring me up again.*
22 Let me thank you on the lute
 for your faithfulness, my God,
 and make music to you on the harp,
 O Holy One of Israel.
23 Let my lips shout for joy,*
 my whole being which you have rescued.
24 All the day long let my tongue
 proclaim your justice.*

Psalm 71 presents well the view that suffering has value
as part of the divine education of man, a theme prominent
in I Peter and the Letter to the Hebrews.

It is sometimes called the "old man's psalm." But does
the author or editor who put these verses together have in
mind Israel? Deuteronomy 28:46 suggests that 71:7, "I have
been a marvel," refers to the nation. As often, individual
and national meanings blend, but as the psalm came to be
used in worship, it is Israel which has seen many bitter

troubles but has been revived and brought up from the depths to thank its Holy One for its rescue.

Even more than Psalm 31, the opening verses of which are repeated in Psalm 71, this latter psalm is a compendium of clauses from other psalms and Old Testament books. Because of these quotations the development of the psalm may seem illogical, and the meter is not consistent. But the total result declares truth of which it is well to be reminded. The psalm can therefore be used either in public worship or in the sick room or as a thanksgiving after recovery from illness. And let the aged continue to cherish it!

O God our strength, teaching us through blessing and pain, help us to discover your purpose both in youth and age, that though scoffers jeer and sceptics are baffled, we may show your praise all our lives long.

Psalm 72   The Time of the Messiah

Prayer for the king

1 Lord,^G grant your lawful ways to the king
   and your justice to the royal son,
2 that he may judge your people rightly
   and your afflicted justly!
3 Let the mountains bring prosperity to the people
   and the hills abundance!
4 Let him rescue sufferers,
   let him save the needy!*
5 May he live as long as the sun,
   and with the moon through all generations!

6 May he descend like rain on new grass,
  like showers that water the earth!
7 In his days may justice flourish
  and peace abound, till the moon be no
   more!*

Reasons 12 For he rescues the needy when he cries
for this   and the afflicted and helpless.
prayer   13 He takes pity on the weak and poor
       and saves the lives of the needy.
     14 From oppression and violence he rescues
       their lives,
       and precious is their blood in his sight.
     15 *So may they pray for him continually,
       every day may they bless him!*

Concluding 17 May his name be blessed forever,
blessing   as long as the sun may his name endure.
      May °all earth's families pray to be blessed
       like him,
      may all nations call him fortunate!*

In the chief Old Testament examples of the Jewish hope, three features are constant: prosperous Israel, "judgment" for Israel upon other nations, and the universal rule of the Lord. Judgment means not so much a legal courtroom decision as rescue from oppression or victory in war. These features appear also in this psalm.

Like Psalm 2, 72 frames the first two books of psalms, which include most of the psalms attributed to David. Psalms 2 and 72 are among the latest in the psalter, probably from the end of the second century B.C. when the afflicted are no longer a class, but Israel itself. As an acrostic in Psalm 2 spells the name Jannaeus, so there may be a play on his name in the unusual word *yinnon,* ("endure") in 72:17.

As is readily apparent, political and religious aspirations are fused in this psalm, and special emphasis falls on the material prosperity of the new era. The oppressed Jew hoped for the golden age in which he would live prosperously in power and wealth. Yet with this he longed also for justice for the downtrodden, for peace in which to seek God, and for a world order ruled by a king whom his people could bless. These religious hopes endure. Like Psalms 82 and 146, Psalm 72 continues to champion the cause of the weak and oppressed.

Your kingdom come, O Lord, the day of justice for the weak and needy, and the time of abundance for the poor, when oppression and violence are no more and you rule to the ends of the earth, through your royal Son, whom we bless every day for ever and ever.

Psalm 73 Whom but You?

The theme

1 Truly God is good to the upright,
   the Lord ^G to the pure in heart.

The problem: injustice, the wicked prosper

2 But my feet almost stumbled,
   my steps nearly slipped,
3 for I was envious of the boastful
   when I saw how the wicked prosper.
4 They experience no pain,
   whole and fat are their bodies,
5 in human trouble they have no share,
   nor are they plagued with the rest of mankind.*

What is the use?

13 All in vain have I kept my heart clean
   and washed my hands in innocence,

14 when I am plagued every day
   and punished every morning.
15 If I had said, "Let me talk in this way,"
   I would have betrayed the family of your
      children.
16 But when I thought how to understand this,
   it seemed to me too perplexing;

One solu- 17 until I entered the sacred place
tion   when I perceived their end.
to the 18 Truly you put them in slippery places
problem: and make them fall into ruin.
conven- 19 How they are devastated in a moment,
tional   and completely finished by terrors!
dogma 20 They are like a dream when one wakes;
                  on awaking you despise their phantoms;

Continua- 21 for my mind was embittered
tion   and my feelings were stabbed;
of 22 I was a brute with no understanding,
vss. 13-16   I became a beast with you.

The 23 Nevertheless I am always with you;
other   you hold my right hand,
solution: 24 leading me by your counsel,
                  keeping me close to you.
personal 25 Whom have I in heaven but you,
experience   and with you I desire nothing else on
                     earth.
26 Although my body and mind fail,*
   the Lord^G is my portion forever.

The text of this psalm is so damaged, the meaning of some lines so uncertain, its order so confused, and its description of the wicked so lengthy, that it is not a universal favorite. Yet verse 25 is "perhaps the most rapturous expression of spiritual religion in the Hebrew Bible."

The psalm says essentially this: "I know that ultimately God is good to the upright, but I confess that I almost abandoned this belief as I considered his apathy toward injustice. I was envious of successful people who scoffed and defied God. What good did it do me to keep my heart and hands clean and then suffer for it? But then I recalled the family of God's children. I saw what a stupid beast I had been, for the good fortune of the wicked is only transitory, and the joy of God's presence is more than sufficient to overcome injustices of men. To be far from God is death; to be near to God is my highest good."

The psalmist does not assert life beyond the grave. Rather, he finds God here. There is no need to put off companionship with God to another time, for it is already his. Man's real alternative is not an irrevocable death or translation to another life, but whether he lives now with or without God. If God cares for him now (Ps. 103), if God is his, establishing his work (Ps. 90), if the eternal God puts high honor upon a transient creature (Ps. 8), if God's nearness is truly the best that life offers (Ps. 73), let man live fully today and trust God for every tomorrow. His hope is in a personal Father, Savior, and Friend.

O Lord, whose company is our highest joy, forgive the bitter feelings and brutish stupidity that hold us from you, keep us faithful to the pure in heart, and in the end, having led us by your counsel, quiet our restlessness to find rest in you.

Psalm 75 Horns

1 We give thanks to you, O Lord,G we give thanks,

Rebuke	those who call on your name tell your
of the	wonderful acts.*
proud	4 You say to the boastful, "Do not boast,"
	and to the wicked, "Raise not your horn."
	5 Do not lift your horn on high
	nor speak with an arrogant neck.
	6 For not from the east nor from the west,
	nor from the desert comes lifting up.*
Justice	8 For there is a cup in the hand of the Lord,
and	and the fermented wine is full of spice.
joy	He pours it out to its very dregs,
for the	all the wicked on earth shall drain it.
just	9 But as for me, I will always rejoice,
	make music to the God of Jacob,
	10 for he cuts off all the horns of the wicked,
	while the horns of the just are lifted up.

The consummate artistry of this psalm deserves to be clearly brought out and widely appreciated. At its core is an eight-line poem, to which verses 2, 3, and 7 have been added. Frequently in the psalms, as here, it is the annotator who elaborates threats of judgment, the shaking of the earth and the steadiness of God.

Three striking metaphors distinguish Psalm 75, lifting up, horns, and drink, all of which may be connected, for horns, symbolic of power, not only belong to wild beasts to whom the wicked are likened, but also are used for drinking.

Not only does this psalm offer good poetry; its insight into life is keen. Where in the psalms is there a more striking rebuke of pride? The way is prepared for the New Testament declaration that the pretentious are put down while the lowly are exalted (see Luke 1:52; 18:14.) Human power is like wine that intoxicates and brings about the drinker's ruin. Better, then, than arrogance or boasting is humble gratitude for the wonderful, if sometimes less blatantly visible, workings of the Lord.

O God, forever putting down the mighty from their thrones, save this nation from arrogant boasts and insolent action, that having been spared the cup of bitterness and the smashing of our pride, we may be lifted up to tell of your wonderful acts.

Psalm 77   Has God Forgotten?

The psalmist's trouble

1 I cried loudly to the Lord,G
    loudly to the Lord,G and he answered me.
2 On the day of my trouble I sought the Lord,
    my hand* was stretched out constantly;
I refused to be comforted,
3   *and my spirit was wrapped in gloom.
4 You held my eyes awake,
    I was tossed about unable to speak.*

Has God forgotten?

9 Has the Lord G forgotten to be kind,
    or in anger shut up his compassion?
10 Then I said, "This is my weakness,
    to think that the Most High's power has changed."
11 I will remember the deeds of the Lord;
    let me recall your wonders of old.
12 Let me consider all your works
    and ponder over your deeds.

The power of the Lord

13 Your way, O Lord,G is holy,
    what God is so great as our God?
14 You are the God who works miracles,
    you have shown your might among the nations,
15 by your arm redeeming your people
    the sons of Jacob and Joseph.

God's	16	The waters saw you, O Lord,[G]
wonders		the waters saw you and writhed,
in nature		truly the depths quivered.

17 The clouds poured out water,
    the skies thundered,
    truly your arrows darted.

18 The clap of your thunder was in the whirlwind,
    lightnings lighted up the world,
    the earth quivered and quaked.

19 Your way was through the sea
    and your path through the great waters,
    but your footsteps could not be traced.

20 You led your people like a flock
    by the hand of Moses and Aaron.

One might call this the psalm of an honest doubter. Its questions are those of Job, Jeremiah, and Habakkuk: Why is the world treating good men so roughly? What has become of God? Has he forgotten, or is he angry? Has his kindness or his power ceased?

The basic verses of this work are 1-4, 9-12, 13-15, and 20. A supplement (vss. 16-19) provides the best expression in the psalter of the point of view of Job 38 ff., that God's mysterious ways are past finding out. But what is the answer of the original author? Does he despair? If the meaning of he crucial verse 10 should be that "it is my misfortune to live in a time when God no longer works miracles," then in what follows he is only seeking cold comfort by thinking of a brighter day. But another interpretation is possible: The author reminds himself that it is his weakness or folly rather than a change in God that creates his problem, and turns to former days, not to be grieved over the contrast with the present, but to be strengthened by the remembrance of God's dependability.

Honest doubt is by no means to be despised; it is a healthy companion of faith. This author is in the best company when he virtually asks, "My God, why have you forsaken me?" Equally every man is in the psalmist's good company when he acknowledges frankly his serious questions about God's governance, and then joins the psalmist in a wide-eyed search for God's wonders. It is better to be honest than to pretend, and to look to the right source for help than to surrender to despair.

O God, whose paths no man can trace, when in our trouble we cannot sleep or in our doubt are wrapped in gloom, let the memory of your mighty works renew in us your saving purpose, that knowing our folly in blaming you for forgetfulness, we may be strong in the promise of your unfailing love.

Psalm 80   The Vine

The vine

*8 A vine you removed from Egypt,
  you drove out nations to replant it,
9 you cleared a way before it,
  and it took root and filled the land;
10 mountains were covered with its shade
  and mighty cedars with its branches.
  ᵒLord of hosts, restore us,
   and let your face shine that we may be saved.

Despoiled

11 It extended its boughs to the Sea
  and its shoots to the River.
12 Why have you broken down its wall
  so that every passer-by can pluck it?

13 The boar from the forest gnaws at it
    and the wild creatures devour it.
14 Lord ^G of hosts, restore us,
    °and let your face shine that we may be
    saved.

Restore
it

Look down from heaven and see
    and take notice of this vine,*
17 let your hand rest upon the man at your
    right hand,
    on the man whom you have reared for
    your own.
18 Then we will not turn back from you;
    revive us that we may call on your name.
19 Lord* of hosts, restore us,
    and let your face shine that we may be
    saved.

The last three-fifths of the psalm (vss. 8-19) present the vine which stands for the Jewish nation that once exercised power, says the author, between the Mediterranean Sea and the Euphrates River. It is this figure that helps prepare the way for the parables that deal with vineyards in the new Testament; e.g., Matthew 21:33-43, and the fifteenth chapter of John.

Part of the psalm's beauty lies in its poetic structure, well marked by a repeated refrain, which probably stood as the fourth line in each of five, four-line sections.

It is always contemporary. Still we pray for God to come and save us, though Jesus came. Still the cry goes up, how long? Still the world is in serious disorder from which it would escape. Still good men are ridiculed. Still, also, we look through the words of this psalm to the light of the world, the source of its new life, and its savior.

Look mercifully, O God, upon your Church
and people, that though the vine you have planted

*is gnawed and spoiled, your hand may restore
and your face shine upon us.*

Psalm 82   Regal Responsibility

**Judgment
upon
judges**

1 The Lord ᴳ takes his stand in the divine
           assembly,
        dispensing justice in the midst of gods.
2 How long will you judge unjustly
        and show favor to the wicked?
3 Do justice for the oppressed and fatherless,
        maintain the right of the afflicted and
        destitute.
4 Rescue the poor and needy,
        save them from the hand of the wicked.

5 You have neither knowledge nor sense,
        wandering to and fro in darkness.*
6 I thought you were divine,
        sons of the Most High, all of you;
7 Nevertheless you shall die like men,
        and like any ruler you shall fall.
8 Arise, O Lord, do justice on earth,
        for to you belong all the nations.

Who are the "gods" in the midst of whom the Lord
judges? Amid many interpretations, two predominate, that
the "divine assembly" is a heavenly meeting of angels and
demigods—the patron gods of the nations—or that earthly
kings are addressed, half-sarcastically, as "divine" and "gods."
Fortunately a parallel passage in Wisdom 6:1-9 reminds
kings, not deities, that their sovereignty is given them by the
Most High as officers of his kingdom to use justly. Also

Ezekiel 28:1-19, in which the king of Tyre falls because he pretends to sit in the seat of God, supports the latter view. The chief objection to this interpretation is that if the death of the "gods" is compared to that of a human ruler, can it be human rulers who fall? Again a parallel passage makes clear the Hebrew idiom. In Judges 16:7, 11, Samson tells Delilah that if his hair is cut he will become "like one of mankind," i.e., like any other man.

Psalm 82, therefore, offers encouragement to the Jews in the form of an address to the proud rulers of oppressing nations. It insists upon acts of justice, deliverance, help, and protection as royal credentials.

The abiding truths here are: (1) All authority is held in trust under God. The rulers of this world who make themselves into gods are doomed to fall. (2) The purpose of government is to help promote God's standards, not to disregard them. Justice and assistance to the helpless are the criteria by which those in power are tested. When God arises, the arrogant, unjust oppressors go the way of any other mortal men.

O Lord, to whom all the nations belong, help us not to be deceived by boastful pretensions of mortal leaders who wander to and fro in darkness, but govern us through rulers who give justice to the oppressed, rescue the poor, and confess you the sole source of right.

Psalm 84   Inspiration for Life's Journey

1 How dearly loved is your dwelling place,
  O Lord of hosts!

Longing
for
God's
house

2 I faint with longing
    for the courts of the Lord;
my heart and my flesh sing for joy
    to the living God.
3 Even the sparrow finds a home
    and the swallow a nest for herself,*
your altars, O Lord of hosts,
    my king and my God.

4   Fortunate are those who dwell in your
      house, ever singing your praise.

Strength
for
the
pilgrimage

5 Fortunate are the people strengthened by
    you,
    in whose heart are songs of praise.
6 As they pass through the valley of tears
    they find it a place of springs.*
7 They go on from strength to strength
    that they may see the Lord^G in Zion.

8   Lord God of hosts, hear my prayer,
      give heed, O God of Jacob.
9   Behold our shield, O God,
      and regard the face of your anointed.

10 For a day in your courts is better
    than a thousand outside,
  to stand on the threshold of the house of
    my God,
    than to live in the tents of the wicked.

11   For the Lord God is a sun and shield
      who bestows grace and glory;
    no good thing does the Lord withhold
      from those whose conduct is blame-
      less.

12   Fortunate, O Lord of hosts, is the
      man who trusts in you.

Because of the beauty of its imagery and its expression of primary human emotions, this psalm is one of the most prized in the whole psalter, likely composed for pilgrims to the Jerusalem temple, where deep longings are to be fulfilled with corresponding joy. The metaphors, however, are not to be pressed too literally; the nesting of the birds by the altars, the springs in the valley, the vision of God, standing on the temple threshold, and the sun and shield—all these are figures. Like birds, if captured and held too tightly, they may die.

What essentially is the psalm saying? It suggests that man is strengthened for his life's pilgrimage by the company which has its goal and its home in the place of worship and praise; that God implants in our hearts the desire to sing to him; that the search for God is a worthy pursuit; and that valleys of tears may become places of inspiration and joy. "The worst sufferers are the best believers."

Hardships as the way to strength, joy through suffering, cravings satisfied, a clearer vision of God, help through the community of the people of God—these are the truths of this beautiful psalm.

Fortunate are those who long for your house, for they shall praise you there, O Lord.

Fortunate are those whose strength is in you, for their heart shall rejoice in their pilgrimage.

Fortunate are those who persevere in trouble, for they shall see you, God of gods.

Lord of hosts, hear our prayer, that we may go from strength to strength,

and fill us full of trust in you, that on your highway we may sing for joy.

Psalm 85   The Kiss of Peace

A prayer
for aid
on the
ground
of the
Lord's
past
favor

1 Once, Lord, you favored your land,
    you restored the fortunes of Jacob.
2 You forgave the iniquity of your people,
    you covered all their sin.
3 You withdrew all your wrath,
    you diverted your hot anger.
4 Restore us again, O God our helper,
    and withdraw your grievance against us.
5 Will you be angry with us forever,
    prolonging your ire for generations?
6 Will you not revive us again,
    that your people may rejoice in you?
7 Show us, O Lord, your devotion,
    and grant us your deliverance.

The
nearness
of God's
help

8 Let me hear what the Lord speaks.
    Is it not that he speaks peace
  to his people and to his saints,
    and to those who turn their hearts to him?
9 Surely his help is near his worshipers
    that glory may dwell in our land.
10 Devotion and faithfulness meet one another,
    justice and peace kiss each other.
11 Faithfulness springs up from the earth,
    while justice looks down from the sky.
12 Moreover the Lord will give prosperity,
    and our land will yield its increase.
13 Justice will go before him,
    and peace will follow his steps.

In this favorite psalm of Cromwell, one of the most beautiful of the Psalter, blessings received and anticipated are skilfully interwoven.

Verse 7 (in the Book of Common Prayer, "O Lord show thy mercy upon us, and grant us thy salvation,") is an oft-repeated prayer of Christendom. But what does salvation mean? In the author's mind, God's love and man's fidelity are to meet. Then come prosperity, abundant crops, deliverance from enemies, and national well-being, but also a state of right conduct and right attitude toward God that respond to his grace. While it is true that some of the benefits expected are material, nevertheless these are only part of the Lord's gifts to men. Underlying them are devotion, faithfulness, justice, and peace. Faithfulness on earth rises toward the saving, helping, health-producing power to set things right, descending from heaven. When God's devotion and man's fidelity meet, justice and peace can follow, and these in turn prepare for his further advent.

Because the psalm in Anglican worship is appointed for Christmas Day, upon it Milton based the fifteenth stanza of his *Ode on the Morning of Christ's Nativity*, begun December 25, 1629.

> Yea, Truth and Justice then
> Will down return to men,
>   Orbed in a rainbow; and, like glories wearing,
> Mercy will sit between,
> Throned in celestial sheen,
>   With radiant feet the tissued clouds down steering;
> And heaven, as at some festival,
> Will open wide the gates of her high palace-hall.

O God, more ready to save than we to repent, whose glory is nearer than seeing and hearing, grant that fidelity may spring up from earth to answer your justice descending from heaven, that forgiveness and peace may prepare your path and your people, restored, may rejoice at your coming.

Psalm 89 The Fortunate People

Introduc-
tion

1 Of your devotion, O Lord, let me sing
　　forever,
　　proclaiming to all generations your
　　　faithfulness.*

2 Forever your devotion is built in the heavens;
　　your faithfulness is established in them.*

The
Incompara-
ble

5 Let the heavens praise your wonders, O
　　Lord,
　　the assembly of the holy ones your
　　　faithfulness.

6 For who in the skies compares with the Lord,
　　what divine being is like the Lord,

7 a God who is frightening in the council of
　　the holy ones,
　　great and awesome over all around him?

8 O Lord God of hosts, who is like you,
　　your faithful devotion around you on all
　　　sides?

Creator

9 You rule the raging of the sea,
　　when its waves rise, you still them.*

11 Yours are the heavens, earth too is yours,
　　the world and all in it, you founded
　　　them.*

Powerful,
just,
and loving

13 Yours is an arm full of might,
　　strong is your hand, high your right hand.

14 Right and justice are the basis of your
　　throne,
　　devotion and faithfulness go before you.

15 Fortunate are the people who know the
　　praise-shout,
　　who walk, O Lord, in the light from your
　　　face,

16 in your name rejoicing continually,
and for your deliverance singing for joy.*

A superb hymn has been supplemented, in the part of the psalm not reproduced here, by a declaration of God's favor to David's descendants. In the hymn, God's throne is based on right and justice; his attendants are devotion and faithfulness; to walk in the light from his face is to conduct oneself by his guidance and help. The praise-shout (see Ps. 150) is the congregation's refrain, or response, often called for by the word *selah*. Today not all share the nationalism of the parts omitted nor confidence in the supremacy of a Jewish king, but we heed the declaration that history is ultimately the story of God's action, we respond to trust in God's faithful devotion, we share the certainty that right and justice are fundamental, and we appeal to the One who can truly raise us high.

O Lord, whose love established the universe and whose justice fills land and sea, grant us the good fortune of those who walk by the light from your holy face, that calling you Father and keeping your covenant, we may know how to shout for joy.

Psalm 90   Eternal God

God's eternity, man's passing frailty

1 O Lord, you have been our refuge
throughout all generations;
2 *from everlasting to everlasting
you are God.
3 You turn man back to dust and say,
"Return, mortal men."*

5 You sweep them away like a dream,
    they are like the grass which soon fades.*

Man's
sin

7 For we are consumed by your anger,
    and terrified by your wrath.
8 You set our iniquities before you,
    our secret sins in the light of your face.
9 For all our days perish under your wrath,
    our years expire like a sigh.
10 *Their span is toil and trouble,
    for they quickly pass and we fly away.

Therefore!

11 Who considers the power of your anger,
    or who fears the force of your wrath?
12 So teach us to count our days
    that we may obtain a heart full of wisdom.

Prayer
for God's
favor

13 Return, O Lord! How long?
    and take pity on your servants.
14 Satisfy us by your devotion right soon,
    that we may rejoice and be glad all our
       days.
15 Give us gladness for as long as you gave us
       sorrow,
    for as many years as we have seen trouble.
16 Let your work appear to your servants
    and your splendor to their children.
17 And let the favor of the Lord* be with us,
    and establish the work of our hands.*

One of the best expositions of Psalm 90 is that of Canon Alec Vidler (*Essays in Liberality* [London: SCM Press, 1957], pp. 76-79): Truth is discovered in prayer. In this prayer, man is restless and unstable, but has a home in the eternal God who undergirds all his history. He is doubly frail. He is not only dust, he is sinful dust. Under God's anger he expires like a sigh. For this reason, at the heart of "what looks like a pretty good show in history . . . is guilt, the guilt of pride, the guilty secret of historic existence. . . .

"This will strike our sanguine contemporaries as melancholy, but how much profounder it is than the shallow idealism of modern man who is unable or afraid to look into the dark interior of history." It is the eternal holiness of God that makes us sad about our transitoriness and our guilt. "A sense of man's misery is tied to a sense of God's majesty. . . . We as modern men have lost both." But the pessimism of the psalm does not make us sentimental or morbid, but gives our work meaning. "We cannot establish it . . . but he can." Since God is acting, pardoning, teaching, supporting, we can rejoice that our guilt is forgiven and our work established.

When Isaac Watts, paraphrasing this psalm ("O God, our help in ages past"), used the term "eternal home," he included a hope of immortality; it was possible, after the Old Testament period, to deduce that if God should allow creatures whom he loves to perish, he would deny that love. Psalm 90, however, builds the foundations, God's everlasting pity and devotion.

Eternal, holy God, in whom our short and sinful lives find meaning, grant us wisdom for the work which you alone can establish, and so satisfy us with your love that we may be glad in your service.

Psalm 91   The Divine Protection

The divine protection

1 Whoever dwells in the shelter of the Most High,
   lodging in the shadow of the Almighty,

2 let him say to the Lord, "My refuge and
　　fortress,
　　　my God in whom I trust."
3 For it is he who delivers you
　　　from the fowler's snare, from the deadly
　　　pestilence.
4 With his pinions he covers you,
　　　and under his wings you take refuge.*

No harm　11 For he commands his messengers for you,
to man　　　　to protect you in all your ways.
12 On their hands they lift you up,
　　　lest you stub your foot against a stone.
13 You may tread on lion and viper,
　　　you may trample young lions and dragons.

14 For he loved me and I delivered him,
　　　I set him on high for he knows my name.
15 When he calls to me, I answer him,*
　　　I equip him as a warrior and honor him.
16 With long life I satisfy him
　　　and allow him to see my triumph.

The strength of this very beautiful psalm of trust lies in
its pictures of God's protection.

Two chief difficulties beset the users of the psalm, the
demon world and the concept of special providence.

In Babylonian literature, demons that bring calamity are
very real beings that must be charmed away by magical
phrases. Some scholars, therefore, find in the terms of Psalm
91—pestilence, plague, and others—no mere abstract ideas,
but evil spirits. On this theory, verse 2 is a formula to be
used to keep the demons away. But it is a mistake to squeeze
the psalm's figures too tightly. Did the author believe literally that the hands of God's messengers would lift men above
their difficulties, or that anyone addressed was likely to step

on a lion? The imaginative imagery of the poet must be respected; he must not be made to wear the spectacles of a scientist.

The doctrine of God's special care needs to be checked by other scriptural passages. The sun and rain fall on the just and unjust alike (Matt. 5:45). God "loves all things that are and . . . spares all things because they are yours, our Lord and master who loves all that lives" (Wis. 11:24, 26 cf., NEB). "God has no favourites" (Rom. 2:11 NEB). The reward of the wicked is not for a few to gloat over.

Is the psalmist then misleading? In Paul's words he is a deceiver who is yet true. He is wrong in his denial that physical hurt can come to the believer. In the account of Jesus' temptations (Matt. 4:6), it is Satan who quotes this psalm and is rebuked. Jesus did not escape the Cross. Nevertheless, the psalmist is right in his affirmation that the Lord is the true refuge, to be trusted to answer, save, and honor.

O God in whom we trust, under whose care we fear no terror and by whose messengers we are lifted up, as we pray for protection make us ready for sacrifice, and save us from the folly of thinking that the disciple can depart from the master, who loved you even to the Cross, the way to life.

Psalm 93   Above the Floods

Eternal
God

1 The Lord reigns,   he is robed in majesty,
  clothed with splendor,   girded with might.*
2 Your throne is established   from of old,
  from everlasting   you are ° God.

Above	3 Though the oceans	lift up, O Lord,
the	though the oceans	lift up their roar,*
waters	4 above the sounds	of many waters,
	more majestic than	the breaking sea,
Majestic	°you are majestic	on high, O Lord.
depend-	5 Your decrees	are very sure;
able, holy	holiness suits	your house,
	O Lord,	to the end of time.

In ancient Canaanite, Babylonian, Egyptian, and Hittite mythology, the struggle between good and evil was frequently depicted as the good god's conquest of the sea, or sea-monster, or dragon. In Babylonia, for example, Marduk at creation overcomes this monster Tiamat by cutting her, i.e., the waters, in two, enabling dry land to come between the waters held up by the "firmament" and the waters underneath on which earth rests. Here, also, God is mightier than the ocean.

The psalm, like 29 and 46, declares the Lord's rule over both nature and man. In verse 5 his decrees, sometimes called his "second creation," are the law. Because decrees are commands with promises, to which the Lord "testifies," they are sometimes called testimonies, and often are connected with the Lord's house. This temple, which is holy, is thought of as secure forever.

History records that in A.D. 70 the temple was destroyed; science shows that the creation of the world by the slaying of the sea monster is a myth; but Jesus bade the waves be still. God is not inferior to his creation.

Holy Lord and king, when the storms of life rage about us and mighty ocean waves crash over us, tell us that you are mightier than anything you have made and that your promises are sure now and to the end of time.

Psalm 94   Is God Ignorant?

God's
rule
denied

*7 They say, "The Lord does not see,
    nor does the God of Jacob perceive."

8 Perceive! You dullest among the people,
    and you fools, when will you understand?

9 He who planted the ear, does he not hear,
    or he who formed the eye not see?

10 He who trains nations, does he not punish,
    and he who teaches mankind not know?*

The
divine
training

12 Fortunate is the man whom you train, O
    Lord,
    and teach out of your law.*

17 Unless the Lord had been my help,
    I would soon have lain in a silent grave.

18 When I think, "My foot is slipping,"
    your devotion, O Lord, supports me.

19 When disquieting thoughts within me are
    rife,
    your consolations delight my whole
    being.*

God
supreme

22 The Lord is my high tower
    and my God my rock of refuge.*

Verse 9 of Psalm 94, according to John Stuart Mill, contains the strongest argument for the existence of God. In effect, is the Creator less than what he has created? Moreover, the psalmist's reasoning with those who doubt God's moral government, highly unusual, is of great importance, and the assertion of his education of nations and men a classic passage. Is not God ruling over his world? If he trains nations, is it strange that you too come under his correction? Do not be impatient, for the Lord will act. Fortunate are those who endure.

Like the author of Psalm 73, this author is magnificent in his declaration, founded upon his experience, of the illumination, strength and patience that grew out of his faith.

O God, maker of man's eye, remind us that you see, maker of man's ear, say that you hear; and when troops gather against your people, or fears and griefs threaten us from within, let your love uphold, your training bless, and your consolations delight us with the wonders of your ways.

Psalm 95   Worship

The
joy
of
God's
service

1 Come, let us sing for joy to the Lord,
    let us shout to the rock who saves us.
2 Let us come before him with a thank-
      offering,
    let us shout to him with songs of praise.
3 For the Lord is a great God,
    and a great king above all gods;
4 in his hand are the depths of the earth,
    and to him belong the heights of the
      mountains;
5 the sea is his for he made it,
    and his hands formed the dry land.
6 Come in, let us worship and bow down,
    let us kneel before the Lord, our maker,
7 for he is our God and we are his people,
    his flock, sheep under his hand.*

There are two distinct parts to Psalm 95, of which the first is a summons to praise the Lord for his rule over other gods, nature, and man; the second (omitted here), a warning based on history against backsliding and deafness to God's commands.

The first part of this psalm has become a favorite for use in opening services. Sometimes, as in the Book of Common Prayer, endings are added that are only partly appropriate. Other psalms (e.g., 100) could equally well be used as calls to worship. Nevertheless, the Venite maintains itself because of three basic truths which it keeps before those who hear and heed it: God saves us, he rules the entire universe which he created, and we are his, to serve him.

Creator of the sea and land, accept our sacrifice of thanks and praise—singing for joy because you have saved us, we worship you, the only God.

Psalm 98 The Victory of Our God

**A
new song
at
victory**

1 Sing to the Lord a new song,
    for he has performed marvelous deeds,
  his right hand and his holy arm
    have won for him the victory.
2 The Lord has made known his victory
    in the sight of the nations.*
3 He has remembered to be loving and
    faithful
    to the house of Israel;
  all the ends of the earth have seen
    the victory of our God.

For men   4 Shout to the Lord, all the earth,
and   break forth into song and make music.
nature   5 Make music to the Lord on the harp,
to sing   on the harp with melodious sound.
              6 With trumpets and the sound of horn
                  shout before the king.*
              7 Let the sea and all that fills it roar,
                  the world and its inhabitants;
              8 let rivers clap their hands,
                  let the mountains together cry for joy! *

This beautiful little burst of praise for some unknown miraculous national triumph uses the language of Isaiah 52:9-10—breaking forth into singing, baring the holy arm, in the sight of the nations, the ends of the earth to see the victory of our God—only now in the psalm the action is past; they have seen it. Moreover, the complaint in Isaiah 49:14 that the Lord has forgotten his people is answered in the psalm by the statement that God has remembered.

A generation or more ago L. P. Jacks was lamenting the "lost radiance" of the Christian religion. Now our more thoughtful observers are deploring the severed connection, brought about by urban dwelling and scientific achievement, between man and the world of nature. Are these two phenomena, the loss of joy and of a feeling for man's oneness with nature, closely related?

A new song would we sing, our Lord and king, a song of your faithful love, of your wonderful acts, of your victories over foes seen and unseen; and if our tongues should be silent, may rivers and mountains, earth and sea declare your praise.

Psalm 100   He Made Us, We Are His

A glad
cry
	1 Shout for joy to the Lord, every man on
	      earth.
	2 Worship the Lord in cheerfulness,
	  come before him with a glad cry.

to the
Lord,
our maker
	3 Confess that the Lord—it is he who is God;
	  it is he who made us and we are his,
	  his people and the sheep in his pasture.

Thanks
and
praise
	4 Enter his gates with a thank-offering,
	  come into his courts with praise,
	  give thanks to him, bless his name;

to the
loving,
faithful
giver
	5 for the Lord is bountiful,
	  his devotion endures forever
	  and he is faithful from age to age.

Probably the best known of all hymn tunes is Old Hundredth, because although Louis Bourgeois composed it for Psalm 134, it soon became firmly attached to the paraphrase of Psalm 100, beginning "All people that on earth do dwell," written by William Kethe about 1569. Paraphrase and psalm are both simple, strong, and as memorable as the tune. They belong at the opening of worship, for they tell how to approach God.

If Judaism had a creed, here would be some of the ingredients of it. The Lord is God, creator, creating; we belong to him; he is good, loving, and faithful; and we in turn find fulfillment in his service.

"To go through life with a heartful of praise, men do somehow know that that is the most admirable way to live"

(John Baillie). Be glad, says the psalm—*Jubilate*. Recognize God's goodness, thank him, share what he has given as part of your service, and for the rest, trust him.

O Lord, to whom we bring thank-offerings and thankful hearts, sharing with others what you have freely given us, increase our concern and joy as we acknowledge you our sharing God.

Psalm 101   Portrait of a Ruler

The way of perfection

1 Of devotion and justice let me sing;
     to you, O Lord, let me make music.
2 Let me ponder the way of perfection;
     how long till it comes to me?
  I intend to act in purity of heart
     within my house.
3 I will not allow within my sight
     any base action.
  The conduct of backsliders I hate;
     it shall not corrupt me.
4 A crooked heart shall keep away from me;
     no evil will I tolerate.
5 The man who slanders his neighbor
     secretly—
  him will I destroy;
  the haughty-eyed and proudhearted—
     him I will not abide.
6 My eyes are on the faithful in the land
     for them to dwell with me;
  he who walks in the way of perfection,
     he it is who shall serve me.*

Who is speaking in this psalm? Is it the Lord? Is it the nation? Is it an individual Israelite? Or is it a prince, as Luther thought when he called it a *speculum regis*, a mirror for a king? Probably Luther was right.

Whatever inspired it, the psalm shows what Jews took seriously to heart and suggests a blameless way for others. The foundation stones of character are devotion and justice. On these are built integrity, honesty in money matters, right use of the tongue, humility, faithfulness, and sincerity. The last verse, here omitted, does not seem to be part of the ideal character suggested in Matthew 5:48. But except for this and for the same note of destruction in verse 5, the psalm is not only a suitable mirror for magistrates but for anyone.

Help us, our Master, to ponder the way of perfection; of integrity and faithfulness, of honest speech and humble spirit, of straight thinking and incorruptible service, of steadfast faith and unselfish love. Then may our deeds show that way, through him who walked it before us, Jesus Christ.

Psalm 102   God's Changing Clothing

Eternal God

*12 You, O Lord, abide for ever,
        and your name to all generations.*

25 Long ago you founded the earth,
        and the heavens are your handiwork;

26 they vanish, while you endure,
        and all of them wear out like a garment.
    You change them like clothing and they
        pass away,

27   but you are the one whose years have no
      end.*

Verses 25-27, quoted in Hebrews 1:10-12 as a reference to the Messiah, offer one of the Psalter's most striking metaphors and constitute one of the classic expressions of the eternity of God. This poet dares to say that heaven and earth, which seem so enduring, are only God's clothes that wear out and perish. By this language men are lifted from their petty finitude to contemplate and receive dignity from the everlasting God. In George Tyrrell's words, it bids us be free from "anthropocentric vanity" and offers us "an outlook into those immensities in which our greatest philosophers seem less than chirping grasshoppers."

Eternal God, because our days perish like smoke, while your years have no end, in pity arise to rescue the cities in which your children dwell, that all nations may serve you and all peoples become one in praise of your glorious name.

Psalm 103 The Everlasting Mercy

Call
to
praise

1 Bless the Lord, my whole being,
    and all that is in me, his holy name.
2 Bless the Lord, my whole being,
    and forget none of his benefits:
3 who forgives all your offenses,
    who heals all your diseases,
4 who saves your life from the grave,
    who crowns you with his tender devotion,
5 who satisfies your desire with plenty
    and lets you renew your youth like an
      eagle.

The
Lord
of
history

6 The Lord does what is right
  and brings justice to all who are oppressed.

7 He showed his ways to Moses,
  his mighty acts to the people of Israel.

8 The Lord is compassionate, full of grace,
  slow to anger, abounding in devotion.

9 Not always does he accuse,
  and not forever does he frown.

10 He has not treated us as our sins deserve,
   nor repaid us for our misdeeds.

11 As the heavens form a tent over the earth,
   so high is his devotion over his worshipers.

12 As far as the east is from the west,
   so far has he removed our offenses from
   us.

13 As a father cares for his children,
   so the Lord cares for his worshipers.

The
Lord
of
the
future

14 For he knows how we are made,
   he remembers that we are dust.

15 As for man, his days are like grass,
   as a flower of the field, so he blossoms;

16 when the wind blows over it and it is gone,
   then its place knows it no more;

17 but the Lord's devotion is always over his
   worshipers,
   and his justice extends to children's
   children,

18 to those who keep his covenant,
   to those who remember to obey his
   precepts.

The
Lord
of all
creation

19 The Lord has fixed his throne in the heavens,
   and he is the king who rules over all.

20 Bless the Lord, you his angels,
   mighty in strength, who do his bidding.*

21 Bless the Lord, all his hosts,
   you his servants, who do his will.
22 Bless the Lord, all his creatures,
   in every place where he rules.*

It has rightly been observed that Psalm 103 is like a chapter of the New Testament found in the Old. Anticipating the parable of the prodigal son, it tells of God's forgiving love, love like that of a father, and describes his justice, his patience with human frailty, his loyalty to his people while he rules all creation. Four times in these twenty-two lines appears the key word *devotion,* or affectionate loyalty, or as the Scots say, "leal love." The psalm stands out as a particular favorite because it presents sublime truth in a definitive form of praise. Man is dust, but the eternal God cares for him. There we find life's meaning; what could give life more dignity than that?

Among the many hymns based on this great psalm are "Praise, my soul, the King of heaven," "Praise to the Lord, the Almighty," and "O bless the Lord, my soul." Widely used in many ways, the psalm represents the best of the Old Testament, not in profundity of thought, but in the simplicity, beauty, and grandeur of worship.

> *Not forever does God chasten,*
> *   youthful strength on us he showers.*
> *East and west are not more distant*
> *   than sin vanquished by his powers.*
> *Alleluia! Alleluia!*
> *   Like a tent his love o'ertowers.*

Psalm 104   Lord of All Creation

Creation   1   Bless the Lord

O Lord my God, you are very great,
  you are clothed with honor and majesty,
2 wrapping yourself with light as a mantle,
  stretching out the heavens like a tent,
3 laying the beams of your upper chambers on
    the waters,
  using clouds for your chariot,
  riding on the wings of the wind,
4 making winds your messengers,
  flaming fire your servants,
5 fixing the earth on its foundations
  so that it shall never be shaken.
6 You covered it with the deep as with a cloak,
  the waters stood upon the mountains.
7 At your rebuke they fled,
  from the sound of your thunder they
    scurried away;
8 they went up mountains, they went down
    valleys,
  to the place that you established for them.
9 A bound you set for them not to pass;
  they shall never again cover the earth.

Food   10 You released spring waters in the valleys
and   which flow between the mountains,
drink   11 which give drink to all the animals,
  by which the wild asses quench their
    thirst,
12 over which the birds of the air nest
  while they sing out from the foliage.
13 You water the mountains from your upper
    chambers,

the earth is filled with the fruit of your
works.

14 You cause grass to grow for the cattle
and plants for man's cultivation,
to produce food from the earth

15 and wine which gladdens man's heart,
oil to make faces shine,
and food which strengthens man's heart.

16 The trees of the Lord have abundant rain,
the cedars of Lebanon, which he planted,

17 where the birds make their nests,
the stork, with its home in the fir trees.

18 The high mountains are for the wild goats,
the crags a refuge for the rock badgers.

Sun,
moon,
and
seasons

19 You made the moon for appointed seasons,
the sun knows when to set.

20 When you make darkness, it is night,
in which all the beasts of the jungle prowl,

21 the young lions roaring for their prey
and seeking their food from God.

22 When the sun rises they assemble
and lie down in their dens.

23 Man goes out to his work
and to his labor until evening.

24 How many are your works, O Lord!
In wisdom you have made them all;
the earth is full of your creatures.

25 Here is the sea great and vast,
in which are swarming things without
number,
creatures both small and great.

26 There go the ships,
the crocodile which you made to play
with.

27 All of them look to you
　　to give them their food at its time.
28 When you give to them, they gather,
　　when you open your hand they are filled
　　　with abundance.
29 When you hide your face they are ruined,
　　when you take away their breath, they die
　　　and return to their dust.
30 When you send out your breath they are
　　　created,
　　and you renew the face of the ground.

Let
God
and
man
rejoice

31 Let the glory of the Lord endure for ever!
　　Let the Lord be glad in his works—
32 he but looks at the earth and it quakes,
　　he touches the mountains and they smoke!
33 Let me sing to the Lord as long as I live,
　　make music to my God while I have my
　　　being.
34 Let my thought be pleasing to him,
　　while I show my joy in the Lord.*

This much-loved psalm, one of the greatest of all, explains the divine purpose in creation, to provide an orderly world which will support life. Wind and fire, water, food, trees, sun and moon, even the sea, all obey God's laws and sustain animals and man. Life's purpose is to please and praise God; man has his share of work and rejoicing in the great creative enterprise.

Verses 19-30 contain many parallels with an Egyptian hymn of the fourteenth century B.C., although the Egyptian poem praises the sun, the Hebrew, the Lord who made and controls the sun. There can be little doubt that the Hebrew was influenced by the Egyptian. The psalm, however, seems also to share the views of the first chapter of Genesis, and is a product of postexilic Judaism.

In Willard Sperry's *What You Owe Your Child* there is a delightful passage in which he describes his boyhood task of memorizing this psalm as his hands moved up and down with the motion of the connecting rod of his mother's sewing machine. He attributes his feeling for nature in the first instance not to nature itself, but to this poem about nature, and desires that Psalm 104 form part of every child's mental treasury. It is the prototype of all praise to God for his work in the external universe—of St. Francis' "Canticle to the Sun," of "O worship the King, all glorious above," and of many another hymn in many a language. It represents Judaism's wider outlook; with Job and Isaiah 40–66, it prepares the way for the world-accepting strain in Christianity. It helps to redeem Old Testament religion from the reproach of neglecting God's work in the natural world, and it provides one of the best vehicles of all time for universal praise.

How many are your works, O Lord, in wisdom you have made them all:
  the light, the heavens, the clouds, the wind and fire;
  the earth, the mountains, the waters, the grass and trees;
  sun and moon, night and day, birds, beasts, and men;
All are yours, all wait upon you, by your word they stand or fall.
Rejoice, O Lord, in your works, and accept our grateful praise.

Psalm 107   Travelers and Sailors

° Praise the Lord

Give thanks

1 Give thanks to the Lord for he is good,
      for his devotion endures forever.

2 Let those rescued by the Lord say this,
    those whom he has rescued from trouble.*

Travelers   4 Some were lost in a desolate wilderness,
    finding no way to an inhabited city,
5 who were so hungry and thirsty too
    that their spirit fainted within them,
6 who cried to the Lord in their trouble
    that he would save them from their straits,
7 so he led them by the right way
    to come to an inhabited city—
8 let these thank the Lord for his devotion
    and for his wonderful acts for the human
      race,
9 for he satisfies the thirsty
    and fills the hungry with good things.*

Sailors   23 Some embarked on the sea in ships,
    doing business on great waters,*
26 who went up to the sky, down to the depths,
    whose courage melted with misery,*
28 who cried to the Lord in their trouble
    that he would save them from their straits,
29 so he made the storm a calm*
30   and brought them to their desired haven—
31 let these thank the Lord for his devotion
    and for his wonderful acts for the human
      race,
32 let them extol him in the people's assembly,
    and praise him in the council of elders.*

In Psalm 107:1-32, four types of persons in distress are bidden to thank the Lord for their rescue: travelers lost in the desert, prisoners of war, sick people, and sailors. Only the sections about the travelers and sailors are given here.

The form in which these sections are cast is shown best by the first: two lines introduce the subject, two tell of the cry for help and the saving act, two urge gratitude. An interesting exercise is to use this framework for other kinds of trouble confronting people today, e.g., drugs, alcohol, bereavement, or despondency.

Words like these of the psalm not only express gratitude, they increase it. Witness the experience of the Pilgrims who landed at Plymouth late in 1620 in the face of many hardships, savages, winter, an unknown wilderness on one side, and a vast ocean on the other. "What could now sustain them but the spirit of God and his grace?" wrote William Bradford in his *History of Plymouth Plantation*. "Let them which have been redeemed of the Lord show how he has delivered them from the hand of the oppressor. When they wandered in the desert out of the way, and found no city to dwell in, both hungry and thirsty, their soul was overwhelmed in them. Let them confess before the Lord his loving kindness, and his wonderful works before the sons of men." Thankful people who seem to possess very little but hardship frequently know how to live in need better than those who have much know how to abound.

> *We who trembled for fear of our safety,*
> *whatever our trouble once was—*
> *we who were lost, imprisoned, sick, or at sea,*
> *depressed and stumbling and faint—*
> *we who came to ourselves and cried to the Lord*
> *that he would save us from our straits,*
> *whereupon he showed in the midst of destruction*
> *his love at the heart of the universe—*
> *let us thank the Lord for his devotion*
> *and for his wonderful acts for mankind,*
> *for he grants us, not security,*
> *but the peace that comes with his service.*

Psalm 111   A Good God

1   Praise the Lord

I thank the Lord with all my heart
   in the company of the upright and the
      assembly.
2 Great are the works of the Lord
   to be studied by all who delight in them.
3 His work is full of honor and majesty,
   and his just deeds endure forever.
4 He lets his wonderful acts be remembered;
   gracious and merciful is the Lord.
5 He gives food to his worshipers,
   he keeps his covenant always in mind.
6 The power of his works he proclaimed to his
      people
   by giving to them the lands of the nations.
7 The works of his hands are faithful and just;
   all his precepts are trustworthy,
8 made to stand fast for ever and ever,
   performed faithfully and uprightly.
9 He sent rescue to his people,
   he commanded his covenant to stand
      forever.
   Holy and awesome is his name.
10   Reverence for the Lord is the acme of
         wisdom;
   good sense have all who practice it;
      his praise endures forever.

In two companion psalms, 111 and 112, God and the upright man are daringly described in similar terms. Basic concepts, vocabulary, and the alphabetical arrangement of both psalms are the same, and they probably have a common author.

In the Greek period of Judaism, following the conquests of Alexander the Great, the law meant much to those who delighted in it, but seemed to be endangered both by Gentile hostility and widespread Jewish apathy. Not all Jews belong to the company of the upright. Against this background, the psalmist gives the assurance that God's justice and his covenant promises endure forever. Study of his works, which are the deeds recorded in Scriptures, and Scripture itself show that he has given his people their land, established their religious practices, rescued them, and is always dependable and kind. Any sane, prudent, or wise person, therefore, in the opinion of this psalmist, will show his fidelity to the same covenant by praising God and by continually studying those works.

Gracious God, who gave us law and a wonderful heritage, grant us so to study your works that reverence for you may be the acme of wisdom in ours as in every age, for your covenant stands fast, world without end.

Psalm 112   A Good Man

What God's man does

1   Praise the Lord

Fortunate is the man who reveres the Lord,
    who takes great delight in his commands.
2 His descendants will be powerful in the land;
    the family of the upright is blessed.
3 Wealth and riches are in his house,
    and his just deeds endure forever.
4 He shines in darkness, a light for the upright,
    gracious, and merciful, and just.

5 It is well with the man who is generous and
   lends,
   who manages his affairs honestly,
6 for he will never be shaken;
   the just will be forever remembered.
7 He does not fear bad news;
   his heart is firm, trusting in the Lord.*

"There must be no limit to your goodness, as your heavenly Father's goodness knows no bounds," or, in the more familiar translation, "You, therefore, must be perfect, as your heavenly Father is perfect" (Matt. 5:48 RSV). Jesus did not hesitate to compare man's character with God's.

In this light it is interesting to put side by side the statements of the twin psalms 111 and 112. (Each half-line begins with a successive letter of the Hebrew alphabet.) As the Lord's just deeds endure for ever, so do men's. As the Lord is generous, gracious, and merciful, so is the upright man. The work of both God and man is remembered, for in each case it is characterized by stability and permanence. And in 112:4, although many translations obscure this concept, the good man shines as a light—in the command of Jesus, "Let your light so shine before men . . . that they may give glory to your Father who is in heaven" (Matt. 5:16 RSV).

Unfortunately Psalm 112 suffers from a lack of realism, for the good man is not always rewarded with wealth, his family is not always blessed. Nevertheless, the man who delights in the law is fortunate, for he finds in the effort to understand God's will great joy and strength. Supported against bad news from without and against fears within, he can be a mirror, reflecting the divine light, in the midst of a dark and confused world.

O God, commanding us to be good as you are good, graft in our hearts such trust that we may help others never to fear bad news, and such a generous spirit that we may shine as lights before men who shall praise you, our Father in heaven.

Psalm 113   High and Low

1   Praise the Lord

The Lord Praise, O servants of the Lord,
high   praise the name of the Lord.
over   2 Let the name of the Lord be blessed
              henceforth and forever.
           3 From the rising of the sun to its setting
              let the name of the Lord be praised.
           4 The Lord is supreme over all nations,
              his glory is above the heavens.

who   5 Who is like the Lord our God—
comes   who sits so high,
to those 6 who looks so low—
under   in heaven and on earth,
           7 who raises the poor from the dust,
              who lifts the needy from the dunghill,*
           9 who settles a barren woman at home
              as the joyful mother of sons?*

This psalm combines in striking way the Lord's majesty and compassion. He whose glory is more glorious than that of the skies condescends to lift a poor, weak man from what we might call the village dump, and to bring joy to a barren woman through children.

As Judaism developed, Psalms 113–18, known as the Egyptian Hallel, or simply the Hallel, were sung at the principal festivals. At Passover, 113 and 114 came before, 115–18 after, the meal. Whether this custom obtained in the time of Christ, however, is not entirely clear, although, lacking contrary evidence, it is natural for us to understand Mark 14:26 and its parallels to refer to Psalms 115–18. The term *Hallel* is the Hebrew imperative ("praise") found in "Hallelujah, praise the Lord."

Theologically, this little poem is important because it declares that the eternal, universal God, above anything in nature or in the world of men, is not arbitrary, but stoops to share man's misery in order to redeem it. The psalmist forbears to say too much, essentially only that God who sits so high also looks so low—anticipating Paul's words in Philippians 2:5-11 about the self-emptying love of God in Christ.

> *All glory to our Lord and God*
> > *from east to west, below, above,*
> *Who lifts the needy from the sod*
> > *and crowns a joyful home with love.*

Psalm 114   A Lesson from History

ºPraise the Lord

At the
Exodus

1 When Israel went out from Eygpt,
     the house of Jacob from a foreign people,
2 Judah became his sanctuary,
   Israel his dominion.
3 The sea looked and fled,
   Jordan turned back.
4 The mountains skipped like rams,
   like lambs, the hills.

God's
work

5 What ails you, O sea, that you flee?
     Jordan, that you turn back?

6 Mountains, that you skip like rams?
  like lambs, you hills?
7 At the presence of the Lord, tremble, earth,
  at the presence of the God of Jacob,
8 who turns rock into a pool of water,
  flint into a water spring.

In form this psalm approaches perfection. Repetition, the effective use of ironic rhetorical questions and faultless balance betoken a stylist.

Even more important than its beauty is its truth. It tells of God at work, in control of both natural phenomena and human history, even when men and nature are most excited. It links the portents in sea, river, and mountain with the Lord's continuing purposes for Israel, for in them he was working to establish a people as his sanctuary, in other words, his abode set apart for holy employ.

The cornerstone of Israel's religion is its interpretation of events as due to the operation of God's hand. Although all things reveal him, not all do so with equal clarity. It is the crises of early national history in Egypt, at the Red Sea, and in the wilderness that constitute for Jews the moments of special importance, just as the earthly days of Jesus do for Christians.

In taking considerable liberty with his material (Exod. 14:21, Josh. 3:16), increasing the miraculous element, was this poet misleading future generations? Rather, he leads us to the heart of the matter, to stand in awe and wonder before the Ruler of all life who uses even the most intractable elements of nature for a great purpose. The psalm helps us to look for God at work, and ultimately, to find him.

Speak to us, Lord, as to Israel of old, through the trembling of mountains and the portents of river and sea, that we may know your purpose in your power, and become your dwelling in whom your will is done.

Psalm 115　Idols

°Praise the Lord

The folly of unworthy worship

1 Not to us, Lord, not to us,
　　but to your name glory belongs.*

2 Why should the nations say,
　　"Where, now, is their God?"

3 when our God is in the heavens,
　　doing whatever he wills.

4 Their idols are silver and gold,
　　the work of human hands;

5 they have mouths, but do not speak,
　　eyes, but do not see;

6 they have ears, but do not hear,
　　noses, but do not smell;

7 they have hands, but do not feel,
　　they have feet, but do not walk.*

8 Those who make them are like them,
　　all who trust in them.*

The blessing of the Lord

11 Those who worship the Lord trust in the
　　Lord.
　　He is their help and their shield.*

13 May he bless those who worship the Lord,
　　both small and great!

14 May he give you increase,
　　you and your children!

15 May you be blessed by the Lord,
　　maker of heaven and earth.*

Because of the father of King Henry V had given him the first verse of Psalm 115 as his motto, after the battle of Agincourt in 1415, the English army sang it. Hence Shakespeare has King Henry say:

Let there be sung *Non nobis*, and *Te Deum;*
The dead with charity enclos'd in clay,

We'll then to Calais; and to England then,
Where ne'er from France arriv'd more happy men.
(*Henry* V, act iv, scene 8)

God's is the glory, not man's; God has the power, not idols; God, the help and shield, is to be trusted; idolaters become like their idols, which is another way of saying that man becomes like that which he worships. There lies the possibility both of judgment and of glory.

If idolatry is both historically and currently a greater danger to true religion than atheism, it is worth pondering the forms which idolatry takes today.

God our helper and defender, governing the destiny of all you have made, richly blessing both small and great, to you, not to any man, we give the glory, for to you, not to any idol, belongs the kingdom, and in you, not in death, is the power.

Psalm 116 The Cup

ᵒPraise the Lord

Prayer
1 I love the Lord for he hears
the sound of my cry for help,
2 for he has bent his ear to me
on the day when I called.
3 The cords of death entangled me
and the pangs of the grave gripped me.
I was caught in distress and anguish,
4 but on the name of the Lord I called:
I pray, Lord, save my life
16 for I am your servant.

Rescue
5 The Lord is gracious and righteous,
and our God is merciful.

6 The Lord protects the simple,
   when I am brought low, he saves me.
7 Return, my soul, to your resting place,
   for the Lord has dealt well with you.
8 For you have delivered my life from death,*
   my foot from stumbling.
9 I walk in the presence of the Lord
   in the lands of the living.

Thanks-
giving

10 I had confidence even when I said,
    "I am greatly afflicted."
11 I said in my alarm,
    "All mankind is undependable."
12 How can I repay the Lord
    for all his benefits to me?
13 I take up the cup of deliverance
    and call on the name of the Lord.
14 I pay my vows to the Lord
    in the presence of all his people.
15 Precious in the sight of the Lord
    is the death of his saints.
16 *I am your servant, the son of your hand-
    maid,
    you have loosened my bonds.
17 To you I offer a thanksgiving sacrifice
    and call on the name of the Lord.
18 I pay my vows to the Lord
    in the presence of all his people,
19 in the courts of the house of the Lord,
    in your midst, O Jerusalem.*

Because of the depth of its feeling and the warmth of its
expression, Psalm 116 has been a helpful vehicle for the
gratitude of countless worshipers. It may first have been the
thanksgiving of an individual for his deliverance from sickness, and then have become part of the national heritage by

its incorporation into the collection of Hallels (113–18). Through its use in many varied services (e.g., in the Thanksgiving of Women after Child-birth and as preparation for Holy Communion [vs. 13]), through its suitability for any who have made vows or been in danger of death, it has become well known and loved.

Verse 12 suggests that with each of the Lord's gifts comes responsibility. No talent is to be buried in the ground. Verses 13-14, 17-19 find that one way of response to God's action for us is to express thanks, both by word and deed, in the fellowship of his people in his house. Thus we prepare for his further work in us. Thus the talent is improved. Thus liberation, acknowledged as God's gift, may become the opening for his further granting of a larger liberty.

An interesting and highly profitable exercise is to study the psalms to discover in them the various forms which liberty takes. From what and to what, does God set man free as reported in this literature?

We thank you, Lord, that though men are fickle, you are true; though the world bring distress, you share your cup; though our feet stumble, you grant rest; and though we can never repay you, you accept our service.

Psalm 118   This Is the Day

º Praise the Lord

The	1 Give thanks to the Lord for he is good,
sure	for his devotion endures forever.*
source	5 In dire straits I called on the Lord
of my	who answered me with freedom.
help	6 With the Lord for me, I do not fear.
	What can man do to me?*

8 It is better to take refuge in the Lord
   than to trust in man.
9 It is better to take refuge in the Lord
   than to trust in princes.*

Source of victory

13 I was hard pressed, about to fall,
   but the Lord rescued me.
14 The Lord is my strength and my song
   and has brought about my victory.*
19 Open to me the triumphal gates,
   let me enter through them to thank the Lord.
20 This is the gate of the Lord;
   let the triumphant enter through it.

Thanks-giving for victory achieved

21 Let me thank you, for you have answered me,
   and have brought about my victory.
22 The stone which the builders despised
   has become the chief cornerstone.
23 Through the Lord this has come about;
   it is wonderful in our eyes.
24 This is the day which the Lord has made;
   let us rejoice and be glad in it.

and anticipated

25 We pray, Lord, give victory,
   we pray, Lord, give success!
26 Blessed is he who enters in the name of the Lord!
   We bless you from the house of the Lord.*

This psalm is a national thanksgiving to accompany a victory march to the temple. The speaker is Israel, which had been surrounded by all nations, but knew better than to trust in alliance with foreign princes. It is Israel that was miraculously victorious when it called on the Lord and now has an important position in world affairs (the chief corner-stone).

Luther wrote of 118: "This is my psalm, my chosen psalm. I love them all . . . but this psalm is nearest my heart. . . . It has saved me from many a pressing danger, from which no emperor, nor kings, nor sages, nor saints could have saved me. It is my friend; dearer to me than all the honors and favors of the earth." How better to start the day than with verse 24: "This is the day which the Lord has made"? And on which days should his creatures not rejoice?

We thank you, Lord, for the Passion and Resurrection of your Son. Through the straits of anguish you brought him to freedom; the stone which the builders rejected you made the chief of the corner; the gate of death you transformed into the gate of triumph. We thank you Lord, that your right hand brings mighty things to pass, and that your love endures forever.

Psalm 121 *Above the Mountains*

To the
mountains
for
protection?

1 Shall I lift my eyes to the mountains?
    whence comes my help?
2 My help comes from the Lord,
    the maker of heaven and earth.
3 May he not let your foot slip,
    may your protector not slumber!
4 See, he does not slumber nor sleep,
    the protector of Israel.

To the
Lord!

5 The Lord is your protector, the Lord your
    shade
    on your right hand.

6 By day the sun will not strike you,
    nor the moon by night.
7 The Lord will protect you from all harm,
    he will protect your life.
8 The Lord will protect your going and
    coming,
    henceforth and forever.

While trust abounds in the psalms and is the subject of many of those best loved (e.g., 23, 46, 91), Psalm 121 is a particular favorite for its classic statement of the shielding care of God. Six times in these eight short verses occurs the Hebrew word which means to protect, guard, or keep safe.

Although in Psalm 125 mountains are regarded as symbols of divine protection, and hillmen are always jealous for the good name of their hills, the entire first verse of Psalm 121 seems to be a question. The key to understanding it is Jeremiah 3:23 (RSV):

Truly the hills are a delusion,
    the orgies on the mountains.
Truly in the Lord our God
    is the salvation of Israel.

Trust not in the hills, but in *our God*. Individual and nation blend here. *I* and *Israel* belong to each other. If the psalm comes from the poet's personal awareness of God's protection, this feeling in turn arises out of another experience, God's care for the whole people. Notable also are the psalmist's references to the Lord as Creator of heaven and earth, his capacity to protect forever, and his vigilance for Israel day and night. These are the individual's grounds for hope that both in activity and rest he will not falter. Although there is no personal immortality in view here, the psalm serves every man in search of help, not least those aware that help comes from the Lord more wonderfully than even the psalmist realizes.

O God, to whom we lift our eyes, grant us to live boldly, free from faithless fears, that in the midst of hourly danger, we may know the joy of your protecting care, now and forever.

Psalm 122   The Peace of Jerusalem

Jerusalem,
place of
pilgrimage

1 I rejoiced when they said to me,
    "Let us go to the house of the Lord."
2 Our feet have stood
    within your gates, O Jerusalem—
3 Jerusalem, built to be a city
    into which men come together,
4 whither the tribes go up,
    the tribes of the Lord.*

Pray
for it
and
its people

6 Pray for the peace of Jerusalem,
    "May your dwellings be secure.
7 Peace be within your walls,
    security within your palaces."
8 For the sake of my brethren and friends,
    let me say, "Peace be within you!"
9 For the sake of the house of the Lord our God,
    let me pray for your good.

Although in Psalms 42–43 the poet longs for the temple, and in 48 appears to be present in or near it, here in 122 he looks back upon his pilgrimage, either as he leaves, or as an old man who cannot go but rejoices in his memories and prays for the temple city. His patriotic love for his people is one with his love for the sacred place, and, through that place, for the God found there.

He prays for security. He knows, too, whence it comes. There is a God operating in the affairs of men whose spirit forever tends to justice, integrity, truth, and freedom. Whatever the oppression in the lands from which he and other pilgrims come, whatever the hardships of the journey, that God is unshaken.

From the psalm, a modern reader might well ask whether security is to be found in guns and armaments, in bombs and shelters of steel and concrete, or in the spread of goodwill and brotherhood. Security is built not by fear and frantic military expenditure but by increased trust in an ever-widening sphere of brethren and friends, grounded in trust in the all-embracing care of the Lord.

The psalm's spirit is well communicated by a prayer of Dionysius the Carthusian, (d. 1471) quoted in A. T. Case, *Seven Psalms* (New York: Womans Press, 1935 [p. 88]).

O God, the artificer of all things which be, cause our feet to stand in thy courts; build up within us Jerusalem which is above; let us have unbroken peace in thy might, that we may always devoutly seek the good of that same City, and may find it by thine aid.

Psalm 126   Sowing and Reaping

In
former
times

1 When the Lord restored the fortunes of
  Zion
    we were like those who dream.
2 Then our mouth was filled with laughter
    and our tongue with shouts of joy;

then it was said among the nations,
"The Lord has done great things for
them."
3 The Lord has done great things for us;
we are glad.

Again,   4 Restore our fortunes, O Lord,
tearful   like streams in the South.
sowing,   5 May those who sow in tears
joyful   reap with shouts of joy!
reaping   6 He who goes weeping on his way
when he sows the seed
is sure to come home with shouts of joy
when he brings in his sheaves.

For lyrical beauty few if any psalms surpass 126. Hebrew poetry is pictorial; here the imagery is particularly happy: realities so wonderful that they seem like dreams, desolate dried-up stream-beds springing to renewed life, tearful sowing but joyful reaping. The psalm's buoyant spirit is matched by the charm of its form.

If the author seems inconsistent, as he both declares God's past mighty acts and calls for help, this double outlook is characteristic of the Psalter. Gratitude for the past leads to trust for the present and a prayer for the repetition of God's saving action.

The South is the semiarid Negev where watercourses are dry and barren in summer, but productive in the rainy season. In the New Testament, also, the bare grain of sorrow must be sown before the rich harvest of rejoicing can be garnered. Without the Cross there could not be the crown. Psalm 126 provides one of the Old Testament's clearest statements of a permanent and universal truth. When God's children are glad in the memory of his work in years past, although they again sow in tears, they look forward confidently to the time of great joy. The Lord crucified returns again.

O God, *filling mouths with laughter and tongues with song, teach us also that those who sow in tears shall reap in joy; and grant that we who would plant the good seed of your Son, the Master Sower, whether your service makes us happy or sad, may be with him when he brings in his sheaves.*

Psalm 130   Out of the Depths

De Profundis

1 Out of the depths I call to you;
2   Lord,* hear my voice;
     let your ears be attentive
      to my cries for help.
3 If you should keep account of sins,
     Lord,* who could stand,
4 but with you there is forgiveness
     that you may be revered.

Confident expectation

5 I wait for the Lord, my whole being
     waits for his word.
6 My whole being hopes for the Lord
     more than watchmen for the morning.*
7 For with the Lord there is devotion,
     and with him full power to set free;
8 and it is he who sets Israel free
     from all his sins.

Although 130 is reckoned among the seven penitential psalms, its subject is God's forgiveness rather than sorrow for sin. The acknowledgment of wrongdoing, implied in verse 3, is part of the larger humility with which this psalmist approaches God. In the same lowly spirit that is found also in Psalm 123, he looks for the deliverance that God alone can give.

The essential strength of this psalm, in other words, is its humble trust. When the person in trouble cries to the Lord out of the depths, he has begun to extricate himself, for with that appeal comes the beginning of confident expectation. With 121, Psalm 130 provides classic expression for this longing or hope or waiting or counting upon God. The Lord's promises will be fulfilled; he will forgive and set free; moreover with him there is affectionate loyalty as the ground of Israel's certain deliverance.

O God, the source of all forgiveness, hear our cry from the depths of our sin and sorrow, and while we wait the fulfillment of your promise, give us good hope because of your love, through our Savior, Jesus Christ.

Psalm 137   Strange Land

**No joy
there**

1 By the rivers of Babylon* we wept
    when we remembered Zion.
2 On the poplars within her
    we hung up our harps,
3 for there our captors demanded that we
    entertain them with songs,
  and our tormentors:* "Sing for us
    a song of Zion."

**Highest
joy**

4 How could we sing the Lord's song
    in a foreign land?
5 If I forget you, O Jerusalem,
    let my right hand wither!
6 Let my tongue cleave to my palate,
    unless I remember you,
  if I do not prefer Jerusalem
    above my highest joy.*

The first six verses of Psalm 137 are among the most beautiful in the psalter in their devotion to Jerusalem, its temple, and, at least by implication, its God. They need not be taken literally. The word *there* in verse 3 (not *here*) implies that the author is not on the banks of the Euphrates. Perhaps he never was. Like the Assyrians in Judith 16, the Babylonians and Edomites can stand for much later tormentors in other places. The psalm is notable not as an indication of what Israel said in exile, but as a classic and beautiful result of a long period of devotion to its house of praise.

O God, when we must sing your praises in a strange land, if in sorrow we forget you and your kingdom, let the remembrance of your holy city that was, and is, and is to come loose our tongues, and in our hearts set that Jerusalem above our highest joy.

Psalm 139   Omnipresent Spirit

The Lord's knowledge

1 O Lord, you have searched me and known
   me.
2 You know when I sit and rise,
   you discern my thought from afar.
3 You test me when I move or rest,
   you are familiar with all my ways.
4 For there is not a word on my tongue
   that you, O Lord, do not fully know.
5 Behind and before, you besiege me,
   and lay your hand over me.
6 Such knowledge is too wonderful for me,
   it is so high that I cannot reach it.

His
presence

7 Whither could I go from your spirit
    or whither flee from your presence?
8 If I climb to heaven, you are there,
    or spread my bed in the grave, you are
        there.
9 Though I take the wings of the dawn,
    or dwell in the remote parts of the sea,
10 there also your hand leads me,
    and your right hand holds me fast.
11 When I say, "Surely darkness will cover me,
    and the light about me will be night,"
12 even darkness is not too dark for you,
    and night is as bright as day.*

Prayer
for guid-
ance

23 Search me, O God, and know my heart,
    test me and know my disquieting
        thoughts,
24 and see if any hurtful way be in me,
    and lead me in the way everlasting.

In the twelfth century, Ibn Ezra wrote with fine appreciation, "This psalm is very glorious, in these five books there is none like it." For it is indeed the crown of the Psalter, the culmination of the Old Testament's teaching both about God and the worth and dignity of man.

Augustine in his *Confessions* (V. 2) helps us to understand it.

Let unquiet . . . people run and flee from thee as fast as they will; yet thou seest them well enough. But whither are they fled, when they fled from thy presence? Or in what corner shalt thou not find them out? . . . Little know they in truth, that thou art everywhere, whom no place encompasses, and that thou alone art ever near, even to those who set themselves furthest from thee. Thou forsakest nothing that thou hast made. Not any man of flesh and blood, but thou, Lord, who madest them, canst refresh and comfort them. But whereabouts was I, when I sought after thee? Thou wert directly before me, but I had gone back from thee, nor did I then find myself, much less thee.

Amos, Jonah, and Plato, too (*Laws*, X. 905), had written that there was no escape from accountability to the divine will, but in Psalm 139 God is present throughout his universe, even the underworld, not to punish, but to bless, not to crush, but to surround and lead in loving care.

At the psalm's end, in a prayer which has few rivals in any literature, the author asks that God test his disquieting thoughts to see if there is anything wrong there and to lead him in the everlasting way of companionship with God. The psalm affirms no future life, but something better, God's love for the persons he has made. Psalm 139 is the psalmist's noblest answer to the wonder of God's greatness and the aspirations of his own heart.

O God most near, from whose love no man escapes, search our innermost hearts, speak through our troubled consciences, cleanse us from every hurtful thought, and lead us in the way everlasting.

Psalm 145   The Lord's Nearness

Thank God

1 Let me exalt you, my God and king,
    and bless your name for ever and ever.
2 Every day let me bless you,
    and praise your name for ever and ever.
3 Great is the Lord, very worthy of praise,
    and his greatness is unsearchable.*
8 The Lord is gracious and merciful,
    slow to anger and great in devotion.

9 The Lord is good to all °who wait for him,
    and his compassion is over all his works.
10 Let all your works thank you, Lord,
    and let your saints bless you.
11 Let them declare the glory of your kingdom
    and speak of your power,
12 to make known to mankind your mighty acts
    and the glorious majesty of your kingdom.
13 Your kingdom is an everlasting kingdom,
    and your rule is over all generations.
14 The Lord upholds all who are falling
    and raises all who are bent.
15 The eyes of all look to you,
    for you give them their food in its season.
16 You open your hand
    and satisfy the desire of every living thing.
17 The Lord is right in all his ways
    and loyal in all his works.
18 The Lord is near to all who call to him,
    to all who call upon him faithfully.
19 He fulfills the desire of his worshipers,
    and he hears their cry to save them.*
21 Let my mouth speak the praise of the Lord,
    and all creatures bless his holy name.*

Although, as we have noted, Judaism has no official creed, this psalm, given a prominent place in Jewish worship down through the ages, sets forth its beliefs about God and his work, his kingdom and his character with more than usual definitive clarity.

This is one of the acrostic psalms in which each line (in translation every other line) begins with a successive letter of the Hebrew alphabet. This arrangement "not only bridles Pegasus, but hobbles him," for the various verses are strung together more according to the requirements of the letters than of logical unity. Herein lies also their strength. The psalm is elemental rather than erudite. The humblest can join with the wisest in praise for blessings which all enjoy and for which all alike owe thanks to God.

From questioning and despair, from wrestling with problems of conduct and the realities of human frailty, the last six psalms, rising into an atmosphere of gratitude and confidence, direct our thoughts to God's kingdom.

O Lord, whose greatness is unsearchable, save us from the folly of thinking because we do not know you fully, we cannot know you at all, that daily we may recognize your loving, forgiving, and generous ways, and all creatures learn to thank your holy name.

Psalm 146   How God Reigns

1   Praise the Lord
         My whole being, praise the Lord

God's   2 Let me praise the Lord as long as I live,
care   make music to my God while I have my
for the   being.
helpless 3 Put no trust in princes,
             in a mortal man who cannot save.
         4 When he returns to his earth,
             then all his schemes perish.
         5 Fortunate is he whose help is the God of
                 Jacob,
             whose hope rests in the Lord, his God,
         6 who made heaven and earth,
             the sea and all that is in them;
           who keeps faith forever,

7 who does justice for the oppressed,
who gives food to the hungry.
The Lord sets the prisoners free;
8 the Lord gives sight to the blind;
the Lord raises those who are bent;
the Lord loves the just;
9 the Lord protects the aliens;
the orphan and widow he supports,
but he thwarts the way of the wicked.
10 The Lord reigns forever,
your God, O Zion, for all generations.*

Of all the psalms, 146 best expresses God's care for the various kinds of people whom the world has treated harshly. It might be called the Psalmists' version of Isaiah 61, the passage which Jesus read in the synagogue at Nazareth. To whom does the Lord come? To the oppressed, the hungry, the prisoners, the blind, the sick in mind or body, strangers, widows, orphans—very much to the same people that are mentioned in the parable of the sheep and the goats. Because of the psalms' liturgical character, like modern hymns, they express relatively seldom the prophetic concern that man shall deal justly with his fellow man. The psalms rather assume that many men will not! But God does, and for all who would heed the instruction to be "perfect as your heavenly Father is perfect," here is guidance.

The author or compiler shows little originality. Almost every verse is borrowed from other sources. But the product is unified, and its two prominent themes are of major importance: the character of God, and trust in him rather than in any creature. God who created all three parts of the universe—heaven, earth, and sea—with everything in them, uses his power for justice and help to all in trouble. This God, no man, reigns forever and is worthy of ultimate praise.

O God, *whose Son came to earth to relieve oppression and set men free from every ill, grant to us his followers the same purpose and constancy of faith, that hope and trust may return with his love and all men praise their savior and king.*

Psalm 147   Thanksgiving

Creator   1   °Praise the Lord

Praise the Lord, for to praise him is good,*
    praise is befitting to our God.
2 The Lord is the builder of Jerusalem,
    who assembles the outcasts of Israel;
3 it is he who heals the heartbroken,
    and binds up their wounds,
4 he who fixes the number of the stars
    and gives names to them all.
5 Great is our Lord and plentiful in strength;
    his understanding is not to be reckoned.
6 It is the Lord who raises the humble,
    who casts the wicked to the ground.

Sustainer   7 Sing to the Lord with thanksgiving,
    play hymns to our God on the harp;
8 who covers the heavens with clouds,
    who provides rain for the earth;
    who makes grass grow on the mountains
    °and plants for man's cultivation;
9 who gives to the cattle their food
    and to the ravens when they call.
10 He takes no delight in the strength of the
    horse,
    in the legs of man he has no pleasure.

11 The Lord is pleased with those who revere
   him,
       with those who rely on his devotion.*

Few psalms illustrate better the ease with which the psalmist moves from nature to man, from the cosmos to human history, and from the mundane to the sublime. There *is* no false spirituality here. Although man does not live by bread alone, because bread is essential to life it may be filled with significance as God's gift, and then is to be shared. Thus at various levels, with pleasing variety, this material gives wings to a mind seeking to praise the highest —not anybody, for false worship is idolatry—but the Lord who controls all life. For these reasons, this psalm is an appropriate canticle for Thanksgiving Day.

O God, at whose command the despondent are strengthened and the hungry fed, whose word running speedily melts the ice of hard hearts, give us grace so to share your bountiful gifts that your city may be built, your will be learned and done, and every outcast brought home to bless your name.

Psalm 150   Hallelujah

Where	1	Praise the Lord

    Praise God in his holy place,
        praise him in his mighty firmament!

Why   2 Praise him for his powerful acts,
        praise him for his exceeding greatness!

How   3 Praise him with trumpet blast,
        praise him with lute and harp;

4 praise him with timbrel and dance,
   praise him with strings and pipe;
5 praise him with resounding cymbals,
   praise him with the praise-shout
     cymbals!

Who   6 Let everything that breathes praise the Lord!

Praise the Lord

Because the title of the Psalter is *Praises,* it is appropriate that a doxology conclude it. The ascriptions of praise that mark the end of each of the five books here become an entire psalm. Its last verse probably called for more words and action than can now be known.

The psalm answers four questions about the praise of God, where, why, how, and who. The answer to where could be either the earthly or heavenly temple. The latter is suggested by the parallelism with mighty firmament, but the former by what follows. As to how, there is some doubt as to what is meant by the pipe. The trumpet is the *shofar* or ram's horn. Verse 5 seems to mean: praise him with the cymbals which resound, first while the congregation listens and then while the people shout.

Over the other questions there is no doubt. Why praise God? For his powerful acts and his exceeding—or supreme, or immeasurable—greatness. Who is to praise him? Every living creature. The Psalter, which begins with the good fortune of those who study the law, ends with a universal invitation to join the shout of praise.

Praise to the Lord! O let all that has breath join to hail him!
Praise him on high, and we all in his temple below;
Praise him for he and he only is lord of creation;
Praise his love, the source whence blessings untold for man
   flow.